The Roadmap to Financial Freedom

The Roadmap to Financial Freedom

A Millionaire's Guide to Building Automated Wealth

Brennan Schlagbaum

WILEY

For general information on our other products and services or for technical support,
please contact our Customer Care Department within the United States at (800)
762-2974, outside the United States at (317) 572-3993 or fax (317) 572-4002.

Wiley also publishes its books in a variety of electronic formats. Some content that
appears in print may not be available in electronic formats. For more information
about Wiley products, visit our web site at www.wiley.com.

Library of Congress Cataloging-in-Publication Data is Available:

ISBN 9781394217243 (Cloth)
ISBN 9781394217250 (ePub)
ISBN 9781394217267 (ePDF)

COVER DESIGN: PAUL McCARTHY
AUTHOR PHOTO: COURTESY OF THE AUTHOR

SKY10071895_040524

This book is dedicated to my daughter, Logan, whose battle with Dravet Syndrome has made me see life through different eyes.

Contents

Acknowledgments

I would like to acknowledge the Dravet Syndrome Foundation for the information and help they have provided us since Logan was diagnosed with Dravet Syndrome. One hundred percent of the proceeds of this book will go directly to the Dravet Syndrome Foundation. It is my hope that funds from this book will lead to more answers and cures for all of those diagnosed with Dravet Syndrome. My goal is to bring more awareness to this syndrome that is such an enigma. You can contribute to the Dravet Syndrome Foundation at https://dravetfoundation.org/donate/.

I would be remiss if I did not acknowledge my wife, Erin. Without her dedication and commitment to me and our goal, this journey would not have been possible. Thank you for putting up with all of my spreadsheets, helping me build Budgetdog, and helping me with this book.

I would also like to thank Pam Fitzpatrick for helping me find the words to bring my message to life.

About the Author

Brennan is a 32-year-old CPA living in the Dallas, Texas, area. He is a husband and father of two girls (Logan Lee and Ellie Gray). He began @budgetdog as a way to help others make money simple. He is dedicated to creating a financial literacy movement and making your life easy when it comes to money. He specializes in helping individuals and families create a practical roadmap for their financial future.

Introduction

Life is funny. Not laughable funny but amusing in an *interesting* way. It is certainly an enigma; we never know where it is going to take us. Life ebbs and flows, constantly changing. In life, there are difficulties and challenges we all must face. That is the certainty. This is true about most people's lives. It has always been true of my life, but it was only in looking back, in retrospect, that I realized it has always been this way.

As a kid, teen, and even a young adult, I didn't understand the significance of life's ups and downs. Once I became fully cognizant of the volatility of life as well as the fleeting nature and rarity of it, I knew I had to choose a path that would allow me to control what I could in a world where little is static and there are no guarantees. I also gained an understanding of disappointments and setbacks which are nothing more than life lessons. Being aware of those things brought me to where I am today.

Understanding your financial and life goals, *tracking your money*, *growing your money*, and *protecting your money* are what this book is about. I have been in your shoes. I have been in debt and was spending money without really thinking because it was just the way everyone lived. Like many of you, I didn't know where to begin with personal finances because I did not have an education about it when I was growing up. I found myself right out of college, with degrees in accounting and finance, and I was earning a decent income as an auditor. My whole life was ahead of me, but I had no real knowledge of what I should actually be doing with my money. I was earning it. Wasn't that enough? I really did not know where to start or what to do with my money.

But I opened my eyes, educated myself, and committed myself to changing my situation in order to create the life I wanted and knew was possible. Now it is my life mission to help others realize their dreams of creating the lives they have always dreamed about; a life that is free of debt, financial burdens, and stress.

With this book I will take you step-by-step through the same process and the same steps I followed. Together we will walk through the framework that I developed and refined in Budgetdog Academy to help you achieve financial success. Through this book, I will provide you with the tools to lay out your plan, *track your money*, *grow your money*, and *protect your money*. This book is going to teach you the same framework that my wife and I used to accomplish our financial goals. The goal is to help you lay out your own roadmap that will lead you to financial success.

I have broken the book down into the steps, chapter-by-chapter, that will enable you to be financially independent. Not all the steps may apply to you today, so you may need to come back to different chapters as they pertain to your unique financial journey. However, I encourage you to read this book in its entirety because many of the principles that I teach cross over into other areas of life such as family, fitness, faith, and business, and are all valuable and necessary to achieve continued financial success.

In Chapter 1, "Who I Am: My Journey," I give you my background. This is important so you know who I am and why I am the right person to help you along your financial journey. I will explain my journey to you, so you fully understand that anyone, including you, can achieve financial independence and success.

Personal finance does not have to be complicated, but it will take commitment and dedication on your part to achieve your goals. I can show you how to do this, but you have to bring the desire and passion to win.

Chapter 2, "The First Step," is where we will look at the psychology of money, especially spending, saving, and investing. It is all about your relationship with money, so you are able to understand your money mindset. This chapter will help you better understand yourself and what you value, which is reflected in your spending. It also focuses on knowing your spending habits and how they are tied to your goals. I share with you what my goals were that led me to this place. It will be your opportunity to hone in on your goals that will ultimately lead you to your financial wellness.

Chapter 3 focuses on getting organized. In this chapter, "Evaluate Your Financial Situation: Getting Organized Through the Balance Sheet," we work through setting up your balance sheet, which is your starting point. To achieve anything, you need to be honest with yourself about your starting point. Let's be really honest: most of us, unless we were bequeathed money before we were born, have a starting point of $0 at birth. When I started my journey, my starting point showed me that I was in a hole; I had an $8,000 negative net worth. So, I had actually gone backward. Yikes! This chapter will help you establish your number, so you will know exactly what your starting point is. If you don't know your beginning point, it is difficult to proceed to the next steps or to have any kind of barometer to measure your growth and success.

Once you know your starting place, in Chapter 4, "Craft a Plan: Create Your Budget," you will now create your budget and begin to get more organized with your spending. So in this chapter, we build upon Chapter 3 and continue my Budgetdog Framework aspect called *Tracking Your Money*. Your budget will help you focus on your spending, *tracking your money*, and committing to your goal. This step may amaze you, as it can reveal wasted money that you can actually use to help pay off some of your debt or help accelerate you toward your financial goal. These steps will show you what is possible with what you currently have as long as you are intentional with your money. In this chapter, you will learn how it is possible to see the finish line even if it is years away because you will have the right tools in place to show you the exact road map to paying off your debts, therefore freeing up your cash flow for more exciting things like *growing your money*!

Chapter 5, "Getting Out of Debt: The Triumph Before the Real Storm," will continue to give you strategies on how to *track your money*. Here you will learn about paying close attention to your money and debt payoff through methods such as amortization schedules. By the time you get to this point, you will be paying off debt, if you have any, either through the snowball method, avalanche method, or a hybrid combination method. We will cover what each of these debt payoff strategies entails, so you can decide which strategy you will employ in your journey. For those who are in the process of paying off debt, I am going to introduce you to an extremely powerful tool that will fully map out your debt payoff and show you the impact that even small additional payments can make to your debt payoff timeline. Then you will be well on your financial journey of becoming financially independent.

Congratulations! You are becoming more solvent, so it is now time to learn how to *Grow Your Money*, the second tenet of my framework and Part II of this book. This is the part everyone wants to skip ahead to, especially if they don't have debt. But let me stop you right here! If you have not mastered your mindset around money and spending, clearly defined your starting point with your balance sheet, and built and learned how to follow your monthly budget, and know how to utilize amortization schedules—how to *track your money*—you need to go back to Chapter 2 and start again. All of the work up to this point is the most valuable work you will do in this entire book because it will set the stage, speed, and efficiency for everything else you will achieve. So do not skip ahead.

In Chapter 6, "Setting the Stage for Your Investments," we jump into information about investments, so you can make sound financial decisions to *Grow Your Money*. Here I discuss the five main types of asset classes for building wealth: cash and cash equivalents, stocks (equities), bonds (fixed income), real estate, and commodities (real assets). We will also delve into topics such as brokers; investment products; stock market basics; diversification and Target Date Fund Diversification; 401(k), 403(b), and 457(b) plans; Thrift Savings Plan (TSP); Individual Retirement Account (IRA); 529 College Savings Plan; Uniform Transfers to Minors Act (UTMA) and Uniform Gifts to Minors Act (UGMA); Health Savings Account (HSA); Taxable Brokerage Account; and Single Asset versus Mutual Fund versus Index Fund versus Exchange-Traded Funds (ETFs). In addition, I will give you investment strategies for building your portfolio and my personal recommendations along with when to start investing and how to start investing. This chapter is about giving you the tools and information you need to really *grow your money*, so you can continue on the journey of reaching your financial goals.

Growing your money might be the ultimate goal for many of you who are reading this book, but let me emphasize that it is not the end. In Chapter 7, "Formulating Your Investment Plan," you will learn ways to protect yourself and your money. A key component of having money is protecting it. This chapter is about building your moat to ensure you don't lose your money due to some preventable misfortune. *Protecting Your Money* is the third aspect of my framework. The overarching ideas for Chapter 7 include insurance and the different types, tax diversification compared to tax planning, trusts and wills, durable healthcare power of attorney, and financial power of attorney. I will give you insight into different insurances and layers of protection. Your action plan here will be to assess where you are, so you can create a strategy to help you provide layers of financial protection.

In Chapter 8, "Build Your Moat," we jump back a bit into physiological aspects of your financial journey and the ups and the downs that you may encounter like I did. Most importantly, I hope to give you the motivation you may need to reach and perhaps even exceed your goals and dreams. Life is a journey, and we aren't always going to win. I encourage you to meet your challenges head on. Here I will share with you my vision and my passion. Hopefully, sharing some of my family's story will provide you with the inspiration you may need as you work through this process. We will discuss the importance of mentors along with some insight into how to prepare for and brace yourself when similar challenges come your way.

Chapter 9, while you may find it somewhat motivational, is really about my WHY. "Budgetdog, My Money Mindset, and My Passion" deviates from finances and goals to give you some background on what, or rather who, fuels my WHY today. My life is not without trials and emotional turmoil. This chapter, perhaps more than any, will show the real reasons behind *tracking your money*, *growing your money*, and *protecting your money*. For me, this primarily comes down to my daughter, Logan (Chapter 10).

In the Conclusion, I will give you my feelings about success, the importance of paying it forward, and the responsibility that comes with having money. Securing your financial future and achieving financial freedom mean that you are able to help others. It is such a fantastic part of the financial journey to know that not only have you enriched your own life, but you are also able to make a true difference to the lives of others. This will be our key focus as we conclude the book. The conclusion of the book is really your beginning. What you do with this information, and how successful you are, are entirely up to you.

Action Plans are included throughout the book. Consider these as your homework—homework to secure your future. Completing these plans will be the key to your success. Reading the book without implementing any of it will not help you on your financial journey. You will need to put into action each part in order to best utilize the ultimate goal in its entirety.

Throughout the book, you will also find some of my financial words of wisdom. These are takeaways you can apply to your financial life. These are rules of thumb I live by and teach at Budgetdog Academy. These are general financial pieces of advice. In addition, you will also find my investing strategies. Again, these are little pearls of wisdom for you to easily reference as you continue on your financial journey. These are the same investing strategies I continue to use. These quick tips are not enough on their own. You must put in the work on the steps and master the framework in order to maximize your success. Don't shortchange yourself or take shortcuts.

Together we will walk you through the same process I took to pay off all of my debt, including my home. You will learn how to become financially independent along with the importance of thinking about your spending and saving habits. I will teach you my framework which will give you the basics to apply to your current financial state wherever you may fall in that process and to which you can refer back to for years to come when life happens. I will teach you the basics, but you will have to put in the work to make it happen. Your why will be what turns this jumble of words into the life-changing plan you will put into action; one that will push you forward until you reach your goals and achieve your Why.

Understanding your Why is important, and it is different from my Why. You have already taken the first step to changing your financial situation. You invested in your future by buying this book and taking the time to read it. Like any framework or platform, there are steps, and they won't necessarily be sequential. But together we will walk through the process to your financial security and freedom.

Don't be daunted by those who question your efforts. It is normal and easy to put down things that are unfamiliar. We both know that choosing this lifestyle is anything but normal. Good for you; you are on your way. Let's begin.

Part I

Track Your Money

Chapter 1
Who I Am: My Journey

First and foremost, let me state that I am really an average guy. By education, I have a double major in accounting and finance from the University of Louisville. I am the oldest of four boys and grew up in a middle-income family.

Like many people, I did not grow up with any kind of financial education. It was not something that we discussed as a family or was modeled for me. I knew my parents had debt, and I thought that was perfectly normal. The closest thing I received, as far as a financial education, was when I did chores. This came about through my mom's envelope system. The rule was, when I did chores that I did not always do, I had to put the $5 I earned into three different envelopes. In the first one, I had to put $2, which would go into savings. In the second envelope, I was supposed to put $2, for giving. The last envelope was to have $1 for spending. That was the extent of my financial education and something along these lines is the norm for so many, as I have discovered in talking with many of my clients. Financial education is not widely discussed within families and social circles and is often a taboo topic, which is why so many of us find ourselves in debt—and lots of it. Naturally, when I went to college, I took out a loan. When I bought a car, I took out a loan. I quickly slid into being like the masses who live with debt.

The difference between me and many others is that I have chosen a path, not the most common or maybe even most popular path, but a path to secure my own future and to be financially independent. This is where my story deviates from the norm and why I encourage you to take this journey.

My journey has enabled me to create my own company, Budgetdog, LLC, through which I have taught thousands how to *track their money*, *grow their money*, and *protect their money*, and worked with many more who have also chosen to take a different path in life to financial independence. Because of my success, I have been featured in several online publications, such as *US Times* and *Business Insider*, along with being interviewed by Fox 5 News, Washington, D.C. Another result of this path is that I have reached millionaire status at the relatively young age of 30.

So why did I make this journey to be financially independent and help others achieve greater financial success? There is not just one answer to this question.

Understanding how challenging and mutable life is, is one of the reasons to be as prepared as possible for the uncertainties and changes. We know we can't stop the changes or the ups and downs since so much in life is beyond our control. To overcome this, our defense is to be ready so we are able to weather the storms that come our way. We also have to defy the culture that lies to us and makes us believe we need to have all of the latest stuff and live among the noise that does nothing to ultimately help us emotionally, personally, or financially. In fact, I would advocate that all of it is actually counterproductive.

It is only when we break away from all of the commercialism and consumerism that we are fully able to be whole, good, and at peace. Understanding this part, the emotional component behind our spending habits, enables us to be more in tune with ourselves. When we understand money, our culture, and ourselves, we are able to control where we want to be and what we want our lives to be like, even among the chaos of life. This is part of the reason why I started my journey that also led to the creation of Budgetdog.

For me, it is controlling the controllable and choosing what I want to pursue because it is good and right for me, not what others or the culture say I "need." But it takes the ability and the mindset to say "No" to a culture that demands we buy into the hype simply because we are told that everyone else is doing it.

That doesn't work for me. As a kid, I was the one constantly asking, "Why?" I am sure I drove my parents and teachers crazy, but I wanted to know the reasons behind things. It is not enough that everyone else is doing it and "because" is not a reason or an answer. I typically am introspective, not reactionary. I do things after careful and thoughtful consideration. This is a benefit.

That does not always mean I don't make mistakes or don't make an incorrect decision. Believe me, I do. For example, when I was in my teens, I thought it would be a good idea to become a lifeguard so I could work during the summer and make some money. I was NOT a "real" swimmer like one on a swim team or who swam competitively, and I am still not a good swimmer. However, it was a pretty good summer job, and I thought I knew how to swim, or perhaps that was a loose interpretation of the definition, so I decided I would try to take the American Red Cross lifeguarding and water safety course to get certified. I was doing fairly well, I thought. At least I had not drowned, nor had I drowned anyone else. Then at the very end, I failed! I failed because I did the wrong kick, a scissors kick, with the wrong stroke, breaststroke. If truth be told, I don't know how hard I really tried or even how seriously I was taking the whole situation, and I really don't think I would have wanted to rock out a Speedo. But failing was rather humiliating! Little did I know how successful and important that failure, along with several others, would prove to be.

Failing that lifeguard test taught me many valuable lessons, ultimately bringing me to where I am today. I really had not thought through the situation as thoroughly as I should have. I played basketball, baseball, and football. I was out of my arena. What was I thinking? I swam all of the time at the pool with my friends, so I figured I could pass that test. Plus, I figured because I was athletic, it would be easy. I couldn't believe it when I failed. I have looked back on that situation many times. It stung! Being as competitive as I am, it really impacted me. But I look on that failure as an important life lesson.

A piece of good advice that my dad gave me was to get used to disappointment. Like anybody, I have had my fair share of disappointments. When I failed the American Red Cross lifeguarding and water safety course, I was really disappointed and even a bit embarrassed because Erin, who would become my wife but was my girlfriend at the time, said she didn't think I would pass it. Ouch! Then I was beyond disappointed when I failed several of my CPA exams. There is more to that story of failing my CPA exams that you will discover throughout the book. But, seriously, how could that happen? I had graduated with a double major in accounting and finance and had been hired by Deloitte as an auditor.

But that is just the point. Life is full of disappointments and failures. It is through those failures that we learn valuable lessons. Often we hear it is not the falling but the getting back up that really matters. That is the integrity and the merit of a person.

I choose to win or at least to keep getting back up when I do fall. Don't think this financial journey is going to be easy or smooth sailing. You might have setbacks or times when you need to push the restart button. That is fine. Keep at it. I am here to help you along your journey by providing the necessary steps for your success.

That is what I did with Budgetdog. The reflective and conservative person I am, I started small, keeping my day job at Deloitte while studying for the CPA exams that I finally passed. My success was not overnight nor was it a financial windfall. Almost simultaneously, as we paid off all of our debt, the online enterprise that I began as a means to help others began to take off. I kept sending out more information, trying to reach and help more and more people. Eventually, looking at the numbers, and because we no longer had any debt, I was soon able to quit my day job to focus on building up Budgetdog, which was growing and requiring more of my time. Little by little, I have built Budgetdog. Certainly I have a long way to go, but that is part of the allure of the journey that fuels my passion of helping others on their paths to financial independence.

I don't know how far my journey will take me. I continually reassess and make new goals, always trying to reach new heights and help more people.

Along with this, I am a person who is passionate and persistent. I am also self-disciplined and committed—not surprising, considering how competitive I am—which are some of the attributes that are also important for success and will help you achieve your goals. I grew up playing competitive sports in Kentucky, including AAU basketball and competitive travel baseball, continuing those sports in high school. Both of those sports, like all competitive things, regardless of what they are, require attributes of self-discipline, passion, persistence, and commitment in order for you to be successful. Those attributes bleed over into many aspects of my life, such as the creation of Budgetdog and staying the course to financial success.

Even as a very young kid, routine, part of self-discipline, was important to me. We all have idiosyncrasies and this is one of mine. It is still part of who I am. Perhaps at times, as a child and a teen, maybe I was a little too regimented. Beginning as a young kid and well into my teens, I always got ready for school the night before, taking my shower, getting my clothes ready, and, believe it or not, sleeping in a sleeping bag on top of my carefully and meticulously made bed. In the morning all I had to do was roll up my sleeping bag, put it under my bed, smooth out the few wrinkles on my already made bed, and then dress for school. I know it is quirky, but it allowed me to quickly and easily get ready for school, be on time, and leave my room in order. Oh, the sleeping bag? Well, my wife made me finally give that away when we made our move from Kentucky to Texas. Keeping the sleeping bag all of those years was actually fairly odd for me because I hate stuff and clutter, but regardless of that, I held onto that sleeping bag. Maybe I was subconsciously thinking I could revert back to my school days to make my morning routine a bit easier!

But, seriously, routine, a part of self-discipline, is a key component to any kind of success and is a must if you want to be financially successful. You must establish good routines and be self-disciplined with both spending and saving in order to put yourself on a good financial path. Moreover, competition, even with yourself, is also helpful when you are trying to *track*, *grow*, and *protect your money*. You will be most successful when you have some type of drive, competition, or passion. You have to want it and be willing to keep competing until you achieve your goal.

Passion is also what has fueled my goals. It is coupled with my entrepreneurial nature. My earliest memory of my entrepreneurial drive goes back to when I was about 6 years old. At that time, my friend and I set up our own bee-killing business. Keep in mind, this was before the time when bees were at risk of becoming endangered or extinct or when beekeeping was a pastime. We didn't realize that it would not be very lucrative, but what can little kids really do to make much money? It was quite the business, too! We had special bee-killing business cards from Kinkos and "official shirts," thanks to my mom. We passed out our business cards in the neighborhood, which was as far as we were allowed to go at that time. We charged about $5 to kill bees with plastic wiffleball bats. We actually made money, and that was the beginning of my entrepreneurialism. My drive only intensified as I got older. Oh, and I quit killing bees, moving on to more lucrative things. Needless to say, my parents told me I should probably pursue other ventures. Regardless of the venture or the path, you must have passion or conviction to fuel you.

Another part of who I am is that I am extremely organized, which is not always everyone's forte. I will show you how to become organized and diligent, so you can improve your financial situation, even if that is not who you are—yet. In a systematic way, I will walk you through the process to help you set up everything, so you will become organized—at least with your finances. Your finances and numbers don't need to look like mine. That is fine. And your timeline will not be the same as mine. Again, that is totally fine. However, systematically you will learn the tools to put in place for your goals on your own timeline.

Sometimes my wife thinks I am a bit too much of a perfectionist and too meticulous, perhaps even a bit finicky. For example, I have a bad habit of throwing things out, especially mail, before she gets a chance to look at it. For me, it is one and done, and I don't like clutter—at all! I get it, react to it, and throw it away. Why keep wedding and shower invitations once the dates are noted in our shared Google calendar? She has reasons that I am still trying to figure out, but the point is, being systematic and routine with details is key to success. These lessons are part of this plan and part of what helped us on our path to paying off $304,000 of debt in five years. Of that total, $76,000 was non-mortgage debt which we paid off in one year. It was the "typical debt" that society lures us into thinking is okay and "normal."

In my analytical, introspective brain, that debt was anything but normal. While we could make the monthly payments, it seemed like such a stupid game to play. It was debt from two cars, student loans, a loan for a bed, and a wedding ring. It kept me up at night worrying about that number because I knew it was only going to grow exponentially due to interest. After systematically attacking the non-mortgage debt, we went after the $228,000 of mortgage debt. All of our "free" money, that which was not earmarked for expenses and was outside of the 20% of our gross income that went into investing, was strategically and methodically thrown toward that amount.

Here again, I deviate from the norm because I know there are different schools of thought about paying off a mortgage, but we decided to do that, regardless of the norm. I understand the math behind it, and I calculated it out. Originally we had a 3.375% fixed interest rate on a 30-year loan. We refinanced that when interest rates dropped, which gave us a fixed rate of 2.375% for 15 years. I still get flack about paying off our mortgage, even today. But for us, it made sense. This may not be the case for everyone. You will determine what your priorities are.

Budgeting Rule of Thumb: Think about refinancing your home if your interest rate will drop by 1% or more.

Here is the part of the equation those who buy into a different philosophy leave out of the equation, as I have discussed in several of the podcasts I have been invited on. For us, it was more than math. Having a paid-off house gave us a sense of peace, knowing that we fully owned our home. It was ours. It was our biggest asset and had been our largest debt. Along with that, because we had a paid-off home, it also gave us the confidence we needed for me to quit my nine-to-five job in order to pursue Budgetdog. The ramifications of jumping into Budgetdog full-time go beyond an equation or a paycheck.

That does not mean that you have to quit your nine-to-five job as a nurse, teacher, pilot, mechanic, etc., to be financially independent. Being financially secure and debt-free does give you the flexibility to make different decisions because you are not totally dependent on your job. You can become "work-optional" and can make some life choices that you might not have been able to make before. That includes staying in your same profession at the same company if that makes you happy and gives you a feeling of fulfillment. For me, the grind of long hours, weekends, and travel working as an auditor was no longer fulfilling. We had a baby on the way, and I wanted to be able to devote time to her. I was able to quit my nine-to-five job, focus on Budgetdog, and stay at home with our daughter. The original goal was for me to stay home full-time with our daughter and my wife to continue to work, but that plan eventually changed, as you will read later in the book.

Along with creating and growing Budgetdog, which you can do in your own way, opportunities continued to open that we would not have been able to entertain before becoming debt-free. Working strictly on Budgetdog provided ample opportunities for us. Yes, there was a component of being able to make more money, but I would not have been able to reach as many people and affect as many lives in a positive way without taking that leap of faith. Our other consideration was about our daughter, Logan. Had it not been for this transition and career change, we would never have been in the position to get her the type of care she needed once she was diagnosed with Dravet Syndrome, which included Erin being able to also quit her day job working in sales in the building products industry to stay home with Logan and devote all of her attention to Logan's ever-increasing care and needs. I'll tell you more about Logan in Chapter 10 and how she has played into our Why. But how do you put a price on any of that? What is the price of security and sense of inner peace?

Let's go back and look at the numbers to explain our reason for paying off debt, if we are strictly speaking about math, which many contend is the logical and analytical components of plans. For those who advocate against paying off a mortgage, the numbers do work out in favor of paying off that debt early. Several things came into play for us to help with the equation and may not always be the case. For us, it was also more fortuitous than just planned. We were focusing on maximizing our lives rather than maximizing the math, but, luckily for us, it worked out to be a positive on both accounts.

The reason it worked for us was because it was at the height of a bull run or bull market, meaning stock prices were on the rise and had been for a good period of time. The market had not gained much as we were paying off our mortgage, but when we paid it off and had that mortgage payment money in our account, the market took a drastic downward turn. Now, we were in a good financial position and could capitalize on that since we had the extra money from the mortgage payment that we no longer owed.

Ironically, we timed the market perfectly for our needs, but don't ever try to time the market. It was just happenstance and without any prior planning in regard to what the markets were doing. So, it was actually our intentionality that helped in this situation. Always remember that time in the market is much more beneficial than ever trying to actually time the market. Neither you nor I have a crystal ball or any psychic powers that provide insight into what the markets will do, so don't try to guess. This is time-proven. It is best to buy and hold.

In fact, to support this idea of buying and holding compared to trying to manage the market or time the market, Christian Hudspeth, CFP, in his article "The Cost of Missing the 10 Best Days in the Stock Market," in *FMP Wealth Advisors*, quotes a study by JP

Morgan, "By missing just 10 of the market's best days, the sidelines investor made a 5.33% return each year on average instead of a 9.52% return that a buy-and-hold investor made each year, *for 20 years*." Hudspeth puts this into perspective with dollars, noting that of the two investors, one who buys and holds and the other who is a sideline investor, the one who holds over the long haul would have over a million dollars by January 2022 compared to the other investor who would only have "a balance of $460,500 over that period. The sidelines investor would have to wait an additional 15 years to reach $1 million" (Hudspeth, 2022).

Again, for my wife and me, it was not all about the money. It was more about security, peace of mind, and new opportunities that we would not have had if we had never embarked on this journey. Part of it goes back to money and becoming financially independent, but it also has to do with life in general and how unpredictable it really is, as we have discussed.

To us, "life is bigger than math." Your decisions, like most people's, will be made around the dinner table with family, not on an Excel spreadsheet. Life is way too short and precious to live it simply as numbers on paper. You will have to decide for yourself how to plan out your finances. Believe me, it may not be a popular decision to pay off debt and to be frugal, or one that others understand, but it will be your decision.

Our decision to be without loans of any kind was not something that came easily or without much deliberation. Some contend that being debt-free means simply having no debt, such as credit cards, student loans, or car loans. For us, we extended that to mean 100% debt-free of all loans, including our mortgage. That was not always easy, and we often got pushback from others. Our families were supportive, but it was interesting to us that some people were critical of what we were doing. The thought seemed to be that they were in debt, all of those amounts were so "normal," so why were we worrying and doing what we were trying to do?

Be ready for all of those who don't buy into your philosophy. Some may criticize you for going against the norm and carving out a better life for yourself. Those who were not so supportive either will no longer be important to you because your goals and lifestyle have changed, or they will be asking for help regarding how to do what you did. You will not be sorry; stay the course. Hold on to your passion.

It is not just about money. The reason for all of this, for being debt-free and financially independent, has to do with life in general, how unpredictable it really is, and your Why.

Think about your life for a moment. How much is planned and how much of it just happens? Company downsizing, the economy, illnesses, cultural changes, and the list goes on regarding the unpredictability of life. These things are beyond our control.

So, being financially independent will provide a cushion and a feeling of security. We know there are uncertainties. Planning to turn tragedy into something that is more of an annoyance is huge. Think about the difference between living paycheck-to-paycheck when something such as a car repair or appliance repair or replacement is necessary, compared to being financially stable when something happens. If you have the money in your emergency fund and don't have debt, those repairs aren't devastating, they are just annoying. Now take that even farther from repairs to more catastrophic things such as losing a job or drowning in debt due to an illness. For many people, those are the things that can lead to bankruptcy, emotional strife, and even depression. And, truly, we never know when those things will happen. I certainly didn't.

One thing I knew when I started on my journey was that I didn't want to live with debt and the uncertainties that result from it. I also wanted to help other people become financially independent and even wealthy, so they could also not have to worry about living a life burdened with debt. The entrepreneur in me figured that if I could do it, then I could help others achieve their financial goals as well. I was already helping friends and family get out of debt, become financially more stable, grow their money, and even protect their money, all through my unofficial Budgetdog time while I worked as an auditor. They were all showing positive and even crazy results.

Those were the choices we had made. I'm not advocating you should make any of the same life choices. That was our journey.

Had we not been in the financial situation we were in, dealing with what life was throwing at us would have been almost impossible. For us, the unpredictability of life became our norm. Logan's medical condition had worsened, and the healthy baby we thought we had eventually was diagnosed with a rare genetic disorder. Like all parents, her health and well-being are our priority.

Life had thrown us for a loop with Logan's condition, and we were reeling from what had come our way. We were thankful that we were not drowning in debt. Believe me, that did not change our emotional situation or the trauma we have had to deal with regarding Logan. But having a financial plan in place and being financially stable eased much of our anxiety regarding Logan's medical care. It also enabled us to be able to move across the country to Dallas-Fort Worth, so we could live in close proximity to a new facility that was being built specifically as a comprehensive care center for seizure disorders.

Again, life's unpredictability was at play. As a parent, it is a horrible thought not being able to adequately care for your child. Certainly there is so much we can't do for Logan, but we can find those who can give her the care she needs because we are in the financial situation now to get that care for her.

Hopefully, your life will not have as many chaotic ups and downs or trauma like ours. But the point is that you don't know what is going to come your way. You have to be ready. That is the constant. Being financially prepared to handle what comes your way can truly be the difference between being able to handle situations and having them ruin you financially. Take the time and make the effort to set yourself up to live in a way that is financially stable so you can handle what comes your way. Let me show you how to *track your money*, *grow your money*, and *protect your money*.

You can do this IF you want it. You have to want it, and you have to be willing to make changes and sacrifices. It is worth it, and I can show you how. You will discover your Why and the benefits on your own. Take the same path that I took so you can achieve your financial goals and live the life you imagine for yourself.

Chapter 2
The First Step

One key part of success, whether it is in your profession, your relationships, or life in general, is being aware of who you are and what motivates you. Part of the Budgetdog framework includes getting to know yourself on a deeper level in order to get on track with the financial aspect of your life, and, importantly, to stay on track. In this chapter, we will delve into information about spending money and how our spending habits reflect our priorities and habits. Understanding those habits is key to being able to change them. In addition, we will discuss how important it is to have a network and team who will support you and on whom you will rely.

Lesson 1: The Psychology of Money

It is important to know yourself from a financial point of view. This lesson is about who you are in terms of your relationship with money as well as how people are so easily enticed into spending money. It is not something we often think about, or some people have ever cognitively thought about. Only by understanding on a deep level what you value and what your spending, saving, and investing habits are, will you be successful on your journey to being financially independent.

Therefore, I would be totally neglectful if I simply gave you the definition of a balance sheet or some formulas to calculate your debt payoff or taught you how to invest without discussing the psychology of money. If I did that, which is often what happens with many financial literacy programs, you probably would be back in the same situation before long. Why? The reason is that money and spending are an emotional thing. Financial wellness begins by looking inward and being introspective. We have to understand ourselves and the psychology that lies behind our spending, saving, and investing in order for us to make changes to those habits.

Our relationship with money is built from the time we are young through discussion, education, and modeling. This then plays into our spending, saving, and investing practices and patterns. As such, they become our habits, good or bad. Therefore, we must understand what motivates us and causes us to spend, save, and invest, to be able to alter those behaviors and change any bad habits or misconceptions about money we may have. The truth can be difficult, not only about ourselves and our perceptions about money, but also about what society tells us. Society tells us one thing and going against the norm can be a challenge.

Think about this. Society tells us we deserve this thing or that thing. Society also shows us what the masses value, such as expensive cars, designer and name-brand clothing, and lots of unnecessary trinkets, without regard to any financial ramifications. We are constantly bombarded by advertisements that convey that message to us. We begin to buy into the philosophy that we will be well-liked, more valuable, or any of the many promised things if we buy those products. We allow that to be the yardstick by which we measure ourselves and our success as a person. But all of those things and products quickly lose their value and really do nothing for us in the end. Sure, we may like the bling for a hot minute, but before too long, something bigger, better, or flashier will come along. The cycle is never-ending. Moreover, we should never allow this to be the measurement of who we are or our success and meaning.

So why do we so easily buy into such hype and disinformation? When we are told we need this thing or that thing, how often do we stop and question or even think introspectively about it? Do you buy into the hype that driving that expensive car or having another of the many latest and greatest things will make you a better person, a happier person, or a wealthier person? I don't buy into that and know that material things will not fulfill their promises for very long. I have never worried about a certain brand of car or have seen the importance of having a brand-new car because I understand that a car does not define me. It is merely a mode of transportation. Period. Since it is a tangible thing that depreciates, we should not accept all of the hype that advertisers throw at us whether that is with a car or most of the other products being touted as the end-all.

That being said, there can be value in tangible items and possessions, especially if you are talking about collectors' items. These items include things such as rare coins and currency, classic cars, trading cards, artwork, and even stamps. These items are on a whole different level than your average Toyota or piece of furniture from your local furniture store. You are on a different part of your financial journey if you are collecting these rare pieces. For the point of discussion here, we are discussing regular items that we consider common possessions.

Additionally, thinking about the psychology of spending, saving, and investing, we also need to consider our financial upbringing as it can indirectly influence where we are with our current beliefs and even value systems of money. Perhaps, along with consumerism, marketing, and the subliminal aspect of advertising, there may even be deep-seeded ideas that play into our ideology behind money that makes us more prone to spending without much forethought or awareness. Take a moment to reflect on your financial upbringing, especially any of it that lent itself to financial literacy. Did you and your parents or family have conversations about money, savings, or investments? What about making money, incomes, and expenses? Were those things to which you were exposed?

Conversations and modeling behaviors about money can be invaluable. Perhaps you grew up watching your parents struggle financially, lose a home due to the lack of financial planning or overspending, or even witnessed them have to file for bankruptcy. These things can have dire psychological consequences on us, especially when we are young and impressionable. Maybe you even grew up hearing that money is inherently bad or evil. The reverse can also be true if you grew up having discussions about finances and money in a healthy and informative way or seeing your parents handle money responsibly. If that was the situation, the outcome will likely be very different from a negative exposure. Regardless of what it was like, our relationship with money throughout our lives is important in shaping us just as so many other aspects are, such as education, health, and relationships. We will not discuss any of the other aspects that shape our psyche here since we are focusing on finances and our relationship with money.

But what I want you to consider here and really reflect on is your current and past knowledge and relationship with money. What is your mindset? This mindset makes a huge difference on how you spend, save, and invest your money going forward. I advocate having candid conversations with your children if you have any and especially with your spouse or anyone with whom your finances are or will be commingled. Making them aware of how you view money, the good and helpful aspects along with negative feelings or apprehensions, being totally honest and transparent, will be nothing but helpful as you make this financial journey.

> **Budgeting Rule of Thumb: When you are thinking about buying a car, use the 20/4/10 Rule which means that you put 20% down payment, only take out a 4-year loan, and have total car costs that are not more than 10% of your monthly take-home pay. Keeping the 20/4/10 Rule in mind will keep your spending in check.**

Let's go back to the idea of why we spend money on unnecessary and expensive things, especially when we are in debt and don't have the money to buy them. But we know that many people, while not financially sound or debt-free, continue to overspend. According to "American average debt statistics" by Lane Gillespie that was published in Bankrate.com on January 13, 2023, "The average American holds a debt balance of $96,371, according to 2021 Experian data, the latest data available." That is a staggering statistic. It is difficult to answer the question of why we incur so much debt; it is different for each person. But affirmation is certainly key. We want to belong, to fit in, to be whatever we are being told we will be when we have that particular gadget or thing as well as the fact that good financial practice may not have been modeled for us. Cognitively, we know that the promises made by the advertisers are not practical, but we still often buy into the hype, sinking deeper and deeper into debt. So, then why?

Action Plan: Reflection

Step #1: Take a few minutes to think about the first thing that comes to mind when you think of money. Write that down. Don't analyze your thoughts, just write down the first thing you think about.

Step #2: Now think about your answer for Step #1. Is that a positive feeling or a negative feeling? Do you feel uneasy or nervous about money?

Step #3: What is your earliest memory or most common memory about money as a child? Again, this should be the first thing that comes to mind.

Step #4: Overall, how do you think the answers to these questions are affecting your relationship with money and spending money or saving money today? Is it a healthy relationship? If not, what are your apprehensions?

Budgeting Rule of Thumb: Your mortgage payment, which includes the principal amount, interest, taxes, insurance, and in some cases PMI (private mortgage insurance), should be no more than 25% of monthly take-home pay.

Lesson 2: Looking into the Mirror

One way you can find the answer to your spending is in your bank account. Look at your spending habits. Pull out your bank statements and credit card statements and take a good, hard look at the reality of your spending. What are your priorities? On what things do you spend your money? Certainly rule out necessities and discount your household bills. You need electricity and water. But dive deeper, even looking into your food budget. How much of it is food you need versus junk food? Do you plan your meals, which means buying only what you need specifically for those meals or do you shop impulsively? Really thinking about what you buy and planning are key.

You need to be deliberate. Reviewing your bank and credit card statements, ask yourself how intentional is your spending? What about dining out? Is it a priority? Do you make it an event that brings you joy or are you doing this out of convenience and poor planning? There is a difference between spending money which can be positive, enhancing your life, that is included in your budget versus spending that is nothing more than frivolous, unnecessary, and due to poor planning.

Budgeting Rule of Thumb: When thinking about how much of a windfall to spend, about 1–5% of the windfall received is fun money. Use the rest wisely.

What about other spending such as clothes? Do you really need to buy more clothes? Is that what you value? Don't misconstrue what I am saying here. I am not advocating that you never buy anything. It is really more about being deliberate and conscientious about spending. Always focus on intentionally spending your money on the things that you value and those that will bring value to your life. This is value spending. Practicing value spending will impact how you spend and how you actually feel about your purchases.

If you really value something, work that into your budget. For example, if you love cars—everything about them—and you want to spend your money on a car, that is a priority for you and you need to make that decision to spend money on that.

Budgeting Rule of Thumb: Use the 30-day rule when considering buying things over a certain dollar amount, which you designate in your planning process. If, after 30 days, you still want it, then buy it.

For us, for example, working out is a priority. We both used to go to a gym, so we always made sure that we added that into our budget. When COVID-19 hit and the gyms were closed, we bought some gym equipment so we could still work out. I would be the last person to tell anyone not to buy something or how to spend his or her money.

You have to decide what you value and what your priorities are in order to be able to make a commitment to your financial freedom while at the same time living a happy and productive life. Don't stop living while you are on this journey. But, I want you to realize that you cannot spend your way out of debt. So, what are you willing to sacrifice? Where can you cut your spending? Decide what you can give up in order to live the lifestyle you ultimately want. If you want to be financially independent, you must be fully aware of your spending; all too often, we don't really think about it.

Those of you who are debt-free and are looking toward investing, keep in mind that intentional value spending is important for you as well. It will help you fast-track to your goal. If you are already practicing value spending, keep it up, so you can remain debt-free and can focus on growing and protecting your money.

This process that I am describing is the exact process that my wife and I took when we first started our financial journey that brought us to where we are today. We took that hard look at ourselves and evaluated our spending. We printed out three months of bank statements and credit cards statements, added up all of our expenses, and assigned each of them a category. Our next step was to average those three months together using those same categories to give us a true picture of where we were with our spending habits. That gave us a clear but daunting picture. What we found was that we were wasting money. This process revealed in black and white that of the $4,500 in total monthly spending, $1,000 was wasted. That $1,000 was indicative of our lack of discipline, awareness, and planning.

> **Budgeting Rule of Thumb: When thinking about debt and pondering how much debt you should have, the general thought is that your total debt should be 36% or less of your monthly gross income (before taxes are taken out). For example, let's say Jack's annual salary (before taxes) was $120,000 or $10,000 per month. Using this rule of thumb, Jack would want to ensure all debt payments were 36% or less ($3,600 or less) of his gross income ($10,000 per month).**

> **Budgeting Rule of Thumb:** The cost of your home should be, at most, 3 to 5 times your gross income. For example, someone with a $100,000 gross salary should not buy a home that costs more than $500,000.

Lesson 3: Changing Your Habits

After completing our three-month lookback analysis, my wife and I realized that we needed to make changes in our habits to make changes in our spending. Primarily our wasted money was centered around food, which was from on-the-go convenience

---

Action Plan: Three-Month Lookback Analysis

Step #1: Pull all of your bank statements and credit card statements for the last three months. Make categories for each type of spending such as food, clothing, gas, utilities, etc. Make sure you list everything, even "one-off" items. Many act as if these "one-off" items rarely actually happen, yet those "one-off" items continue to plague them in different forms forever.

Step #2: Drill down even further to include not just food, but subcategories such as groceries, on-the-go food purchases, and dining out.

Step #3: Average each category for the three months. You will be able to see what your spending habits are, see the Resources. If you are tech savvy, you may even want to create a pie chart. It is a great visual.

Step #4: Evaluate your spending to assess if you have wasted money. What are you doing with the excess if there is any? Now see where you can adjust. See the template in Figure 2.1.

(continued)

(continued)

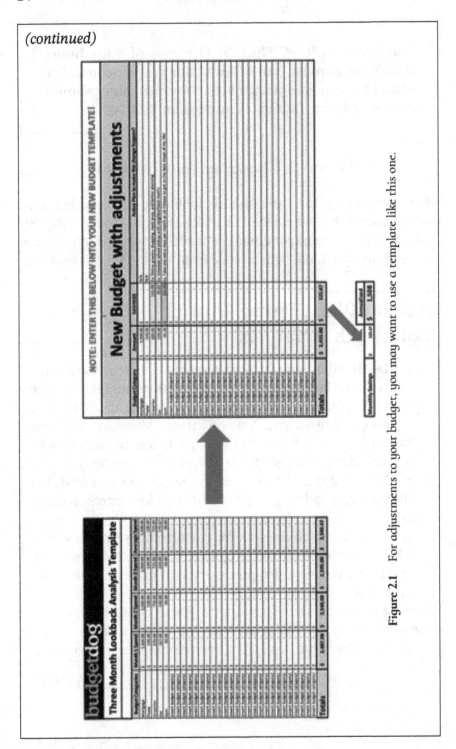

Figure 2.1   For adjustments to your budget, you may want to use a template like this one.

food purchases; it was nothing more than poor forethought and planning. Changing our habits meant being able to change that wasteful spending into savings. Since we were focused at that time on trying to pay off my student loans, we also realized that we could take that $1,000 we were wasting on convenience food purchases and apply it to that particular debt. In addition, by using an amortization schedule, we realized that by applying that $1,000 a month to my regular monthly student loans payments, we could shorten the student debt payoff timeline to six months. An amortization schedule is a calculation that allows you to see the amount of money you pay in principal as well as the amount of money from each payment that you actually pay in interest over a designated period of time. Paying toward the principal and shortening the amount of time saves on the amount you will pay in interest.

With this realization, we immediately became more disciplined, so we could more expediently meet our goal and even save money by paying off the debt faster and therefore knocking off some of the interest. But it was actually making the time to look at our spending that was necessary and eye-opening.

Tapping into yourself and taking that hard look in the mirror is difficult but fundamental in understanding who you really are, so you can ultimately be successful with the goal at hand. That is why every student enrolled in Budgetdog Academy meets with a behavioral psychologist. This is key to helping each person understand individually his or her negative cognitions, so each one is better able to know what is holding him or her back from reaching personal goals.

Rarely is it simply one's lifestyle or income alone. In fact, according to a 2023 study conducted by Ramsey Solutions, those who are millionaires aren't all in high-paying positions. This same study notes that "Only 31% averaged $100,000 a year over the course of their career, and one-third never made six figures *in any single working year* of their career."

Society wants us to think it is a person's lifestyle or income that causes the individual to be in debt or to make irrational financial decisions. Statistics show us otherwise. More accurately, it is people's expectations of their intended lifestyle and their unwillingness to sacrifice that are the root and cause. Meeting with the behavioral psychologist and understanding spending habits and the reason behind them are a fundamental part of my Budgetdog Academy Framework. After that, you are able to make different decisions about your spending, being disciplined and focused rather than reactionary.

Also key to this self-evaluation is understanding when and how you spend. Now that you know what you spend your money on, think about when and why, so you can change that spending habit. Are your purchases made because you think they will make things easier, such as running through fast food restaurants for morning coffee, breakfast, lunch, dinner, or all of them? As I pointed out from the process that my wife and I went through, $1,000 of our spending was wasted on just that. Maybe you buy things, spending unnecessary money as an emotional response. Many people do exactly that. In fact, a 2021 study by *PNC Insights* "Emotional Spending: Learn What it is and How to Control It," indicates that almost half "of Americans say emotions have caused them to spend more than they can reasonably afford."

There is a psychology that is behind emotional spending. It can be due to emotions ranging from sadness, which could be from failed relationships, personal insecurities, and/or financial worries, all the way to positive emotions like excitement. If you discover that some or most of your own spending is due to emotional spending, you might be interested in tapping more into the psychology behind it. There is a host of information published about this topic. One quick read that you might enjoy is "What Is Emotional Spending?" by Marianne Hayes (2023).

Nonetheless, we know that emotional and impulse buying drives up sales. Companies and stores bank on that. We see something we like, so we buy it. We don't think about it; we just want it and buy it. You need to train yourself in order to change your spending habits. Remember you are trying to break those spending habits so really think about that purchase.

Budgeting Rule of Thumb for Saving and Investing: Use the 50/30/20 rule, which states that you allocate 30% spend on your wants, 50% spend on your necessities, and 20% spend on saving/investing.

Do you need it? Need and want are totally different things. My wife is not an impulsive shopper. One reason is because, as she was growing up, she was trained to think about each purchase. The rule was that she had to think about what she wanted to buy for at least 24 hours. Secondarily, she had to calculate how long she would have to work to pay for the item she wanted. Often, after doing both of those things, she would decide that she really did not want it that badly nor did she need it. Challenge yourself to think about your purchases and spending habits. Carefully calculate the amount of money you are laying out for the purchases. Also, think about whether or not this will sidetrack you from your goal. You have to commit to the goal at hand.

Budgeting Rule of Thumb: When buying a car, keep in mind that the total lifetime cost of a car should be calculated as the sticker price times 3.

Action Plan: Make Changes

Step #1: Have a very real conversation about money and finances with your partner if you have a significant person who will also be involved with your finances. It will be extremely difficult if one of you is not buying into the goal of being debt-free. If your finances are commingled, you both need to be resolute regarding the goal at hand.

(continued)

(continued)

Step #2: Part of the conversation, either on your own or involving your partner, is to be able to understand your spending habits.

Step #3: Know your goal and stay focused on that goal. As previously mentioned, make the goal real. Write it down. It has to be tangible. Commit to it. Make it highly visible. I use a whiteboard, which makes its way into the living room often. I think it goes with the decor, but my wife doesn't approve. You will have to find what works best for you.

Lesson 4: Building a Support Team

For some people, sticking to a goal is easier than for others. Whichever category you are in, I am on your side; I am your cheerleader and will help you along your journey. Having a mentor alongside to help guide you is nothing more than practical advice. With most endeavors, having someone who can help encourage, guide, and inspire you is a huge advantage. Think about running, weight loss, or careers, for example. Key to the success in these endeavors as well as so many others is having a mentor to help guide you along the path.

Often the path is difficult and tiring. Having a mentor who has real experience and who personally knows the pitfalls and the challenges will keep you on that path. A good mentor will keep you from quitting and will help you continue to make strides toward your goal. Finding a mentor may entail a fee. You need to think about it as an investment rather than an expense. Invest in yourself. Invest in your future. Change your course now and set yourself up for future success. Chances are, it will be easier and less costly overall if you invest in a good mentor. I know the pitfalls and the challenges. I was in the same situation as you are not that long ago; I understand.

I do the same thing that I am suggesting to you. I have three mentors who I pay a pretty penny to help with my business. There are things on the business side that are out of my wheelhouse and are not my area of expertise. I rely on these three mentors to help guide me. The price is worth it. As a result of bringing them on board, my business has multiplied, so the rate of investment has been well worth the price. I walk the walk. I am not telling you to do anything I don't do myself or don't believe in firmly and with conviction.

Think about your own situation. For me, I don't hesitate spending money on mentorships because it seamlessly speeds up the process. Keep in mind that there are two types of currencies. The first is money. The second is time. You will need to decide which one makes more sense in regard to a mentor. Ultimately, I think you will reap both time and money by using a good mentor.

Along with a committed mentor, it is important to have a supportive community. Defining community is a subjective thing. But, importantly, surrounding yourself with like-minded people can be a key component to success. Stay tapped into blogs and podcasts that further your agenda and keep you on track with your goal. Others will try to tear you down. Remember the goal at hand. It is not immediate, but keeping it in mind and setting some goals that are imminent will help you stay focused and committed. Remember you wrote it down and put it in a visible spot such as my whiteboard to remind you daily about your goals.

Also, try to steer clear of those who try to distract you. Sometimes just looking back at bank statements and credit card statements, again being introspective, we can see how often we are enticed and even cajoled by others into spending. When you are going through this process, ask yourself how often your friends and family are involved with you spending money. Further, will they be supportive when you tell them you are not buying this thing or not going to a certain place because it is not in your budget?

I was lucky to have the undying support of my wife. She and our families were our community. Our community actually became very small during our process. In fact, we surprisingly lost many of our "closest friends." When we became focused on our careers and became deeply committed to our financial goals, we were shunned. We were no longer invited to hang out with the group that had been such an integral part of our lives in high school and in college; we were no longer invited to parties, showers, or even weddings. Mostly this will come as a result of a shift in your goals. At that time, our goal was to stay on our debt-free journey, but their journey was not the same. It is not wrong or right, just different which became divergent. Being ostracized presented an emotional and mental challenge. Yes, our families supported our endeavor, but it really and finally came down to Erin and me. Her determination and encouragement coupled with her commitment were key to our financial health and success. Keep reminding yourself of your goal at hand and keep focused on your visual reminder of it.

Discussing our long-term goals and dreams, many of them requiring money, stability, and financial independence, was really the catalyst for us being able to be committed as a couple and stay focused on our goals. There were times in the very beginning when even Erin's commitment was not 100%, nor was her commitment an instantaneous thing. Part of that was my fault. At first, I approached things as I do with almost everything, in a very analytical way, charting out our entire life on spreadsheets. The more she pushed back telling me to chill with all of my spreadsheets, the more I dug in, creating even more and more spreadsheets as if that would win her over and make her immediately see all of the numbers like I was seeing them. It wasn't until we began to have serious conversations about the life we wanted, a vision we both shared, which became our why and our reason, that she was able to commit to our financial journey.

Then Erin was enlightened with the same things I was actually trying to convince her about through the numbers on my spreadsheets, but she was beginning to put everything together and see things through a different lens, thus getting on board with our goal. She had come to things her own way rather than by me forcing everything on her in such a methodical and, to her, boring and overwhelming way. It wasn't until we began to have serious conversations about the life we wanted, a vision we both shared, which became our why and our reason, that she was able to commit to our financial journey. Once committed, she was all in and the journey became far easier. And then, she was fired up. When she heard that others were so successfully doing what we wanted to do and understood the overall plan, we were a team, each being a mentor and guide for the other person. For us, this was key.

Action Plan: Build Support and Encouragement

Step #1: Tune in to financial podcasts. I often left these on in the car as we were driving, knowing they were saying the same things I was trying to get across to Erin. Hearing them from others seemed to make more sense, at least to her. Even if you are just listening to them for yourself, they are insightful and encouraging.

Step #2: Be careful of your approach if you are trying to get others onboard with you. For example, my aggressive, analytical approach did not work for Erin, and she certainly did not connect with all of my extensive amount of spreadsheets, even though I thought they were amazing! I also tried a bit of subliminal persuasion at the same time by listening to podcasts such as Dave Ramsey, the financial advisor, when we were in the car. Instead, I had to appeal to Erin's dreams and goals. I would suggest you try a big picture approach, especially if you are dealing with others. How to get to that end place will come later, but you need to understand where you are trying to get to first.

Lesson 5: Staying the Course

This will not always be easy. Ninety-two percent of people who take on a new endeavor will fail. In an article written by Marcel Schwantes et al. (2018), who is the contributing editor and founder of *Leadership from the Core*, published in *Inc.* magazine, he noted that since 92% are not successful, "That leaves 8 percent of us in a very elite category of goal-achievers." The important thing to consider is how to be in the 8%. What can you do to improve your odds and your success rate?

We became part of the 8% because together we budgeted, planned, saved, and finally achieved each goal that we set. It took a lot of effort from both of us, but we were stronger together. We were both deeply committed to paying off all of the debt and not accumulating more debt. We stuck to our financial plan, reminding each other often of the end goal and our dreams.

An interesting and positive unintended side-effect was that overall our lives improved, too. It really was a consequence of budgeting. We set our budget and still don't deviate from it, including our food budget. To minimize our food budget, we look to see what is on sale and plan our meals accordingly. Before we started on our financial journey, we simply went to the grocery store. But once we were on our financial journey, to ensure that we stayed within our food budget, we calculated what was a reasonable amount to spend on groceries in a month, which for us was $600 at the time. Then we broke that down to $150 per week. It was easy math.

The Kroger Clicklist was the best way for us to stay within that $150 per week limit because we could check our final spending before we clicked the checkout button. We could eliminate anything unnecessary or over the budget. Not only was it easy math, but it also provided us with control. We still do the same thing today. We don't buy extras or junk food. Sunday is our food prep day. Again, everything is calculated. But because we cut out all of the extra junk that we didn't need and is nothing more than empty calories, we became even healthier. Well, we cut out almost everything. Truth be told, occasionally, I eventually discovered, mascara from the grocery store found its way onto the Clicklist! Creative, I suppose, but I can't really complain because Erin always stayed within the budget and went without something from the store, so she could have her mascara. But the point is that since we are like-minded regarding our financial philosophies, success was easy.

Budgeting Rule of Thumb: In order to figure out how much you should spend on food for groceries and dining out, typically it should be between 10–15% of your gross income.

I am a person who needs to know the endgame. Part of that may be due to my competitive nature and part is due to being so methodical. This is nothing new to who I am. For example, my wife and I started dating when we were in high school. We continued to date in college. Our goal was eventually to get married. But I needed to make sure I was able to fully commit myself to her.

The emotional side of me could have been more rash, jumping into marriage sooner since we had already been together for such a long time, had graduated college, and had started careers. But the logical side of me knew I needed to wait until I was ready. My ready meant being financially stable in a career. I needed to be able to provide Erin with stability. It was not that she didn't already have a career and wasn't self-sufficient, but I needed to be able to enter marriage confidently and securely.

Actually, I didn't really understand what all of that meant. I had yet to fully figure out life after college. It seemed so daunting, and I didn't even know all of the right questions to ask. Remember, I did not come from a family who discussed finances. So I began asking questions. Surprising that I would do that, right? I bombarded my dad and others with questions about mortgages, insurance, living expenses, car payments; the list was endless. The more answers I got, the more questions I asked. I continued to collect data and eventually set a timeline for when I knew I would be able to get married.

That is the same thing that applies here with financial goals. Being introspective, asking questions, and setting realistic, attainable, and logical goals will lead you to success. Together, I will help you create that timeline—logically and systematically, which will be your roadmap for success.

For me, I knew I did not want to live week by week, paycheck to paycheck, and be beholden to the whims of others. I wanted to control my family's destiny. Again, the questioner in me began to challenge the deep-rooted belief system that I grew up in that plays to the idea that stuff is important and everyone is in debt. I can't and don't buy into that philosophy. Mathematically, you can't build wealth if you have bad debt. Until you are debt-free from credit cards, of which an "average credit card interest rate is 24.14%, according to Forbes Advisor's weekly credit card rates report" or a car loan with interest rates ranging from "6.07 percent for new cars and 10.26 percent for used" cars (Betterton, 2023) as, according to the fourth quarter data from Experian, you will remain in debt. I needed the stability and security of owning my own cars and home, making my money work for me, working smarter rather than longer and harder, and being totally debt-free in order to best provide for my family. That is key to my Why, and which is going to be different from your reasons. It doesn't matter what your reasons are or your Why, just know it and own it. Make it real. Use a picture that helps show you what your aspirations are.

Here is part of my WHY (Figure 2.2).

I tell my clients that my method will work. It is a guarantee provided they work and put forth the effort. If you don't commit and stick to the plan, you will not be successful. That is a guarantee and an unfortunate fact. Think about it this way. The athletic part of me who is diligent about working out and eating well to fuel my body in a healthy way knows emphatically that if I don't go to the gym but rather sleep in and put off working out for sometime in the future, and I go to Wendy's or any other number of fast food places rather than eating nutritional food, I will not be fit. Instead, I will become more and more out of shape and more and more unhealthy. You can't eat cookies and donuts and be fit and trim. It is the same way with a financial plan. Lip service without commitment and action is a total waste of time. You need to reflect on whether or not you can be onboard 100%. It isn't something you can do *sort of*. That is not to say you may not have to make adjustments to your budget and

Figure 2.2

tweak your financial plans along the way. However, make a commitment to be resolute and steadfast, so you will see success.

I want to also stress the fact that it is totally fine to go against the masses. What you are doing by becoming fiscally responsible, getting out of debt, investing, and becoming financially successful is not the norm. In that fact alone, you are rebelling against a society that buys into having stuff, getting into debt for lots of unnecessary things, as if any of it will make people truly happy, yet never owning any of it because it is actually unpaid for. Therefore, as you reflect on your spending and spending habits, your value system, your support system, and your reasons, consider how unique and individual you are. That alone counts for so much and will help you along your journey. My question to you now is, are you deeply committed and ready to embark on an exciting and fulfilling financial journey? Have you completed your action plans? If not, go back and complete the action plans. If so, then let's move forward.

Action Plan: Detailing Out Your Financial Plan and Changes

Step #1: Setting forth your financial plan is key to seeing your end goal to fruition. Your first plan of action is to write out your goals.

Step #2: Ask yourself what your ideal life looks like in terms of your finances. Also consider when you REALISTICALLY want to hit this goal/goals. Write these down. Make them permanent.

Step #3: Automate all payments, investments, and debt payoffs you can, so you do not have to actively think about them. This is a time saver and a way to simplify your life. Turn on autopay for everything that you can.

Step #4: Develop systems that work for you to make sure you stay consistent. This may take some trial and error to find the systems or methods that work best for you. Don't give up. Keep tweaking them until they become a habit.

Step #5: Try using your phone calendar for your reminders. For example, I use my iPhone calendar to remind me about my water bottle. I have a water bottle that is 25 ounces. I know if I want to make sure I drink 125 ounces of water a day, my goal, I need to fill it up five times. If I don't make note of that and update it to keep track of how many times I actually have filled it up, I will forget about it and/or lose track of how much I have actually consumed.

Step #6: Start small. Prioritize a few goals that you want to accomplish each day. Don't try to take on too much and overwhelm yourself. My mother-in-law often reminded Erin and her siblings how to eat an elephant whenever they had big tasks at hand. Their response always was "One bite at a time." In other words, do this a little at a time. You can't eat an elephant in one bite nor can you change all of your habits at once. Start small to see success.

Chapter 3

Evaluate Your Financial Situation: Getting Organized Through the Balance Sheet

Now that you have a better understanding of your goals, your spending habits, and the reasons why you want to make this financial journey, it is time to take a look at your current financial position so you can organize your financial plan. In order to do this, you will need a balance sheet. While most people begin their financial journey with a budget (and usually only a budget sadly), I ALWAYS recommend to begin with a balance sheet. This may seem different than most basic financial programs out there as many will teach you only how to budget. However, coming from a CPA corporate background at Deloitte and seeing how hundreds of large and successful companies operate, it became obvious to me that everyone needs to begin with a balance sheet. I love working out, so I always compare a balance sheet to working out. If you walk into a gym without any understanding of your current body weight, how will you know which workouts to do? What is your starting weight and what are your personal goals? Are you trying to lose weight? Are you trying to gain muscle or are you trying to maintain your weight? If you rush into budgeting, you have rushed into working out without a plan. No matter how hard you are working, you are not working smart and in line with your specific goals. This is why we will begin your financial journey with a balance sheet and then later cover budgeting in Chapter 4. A balance sheet will serve as one of your three core financial statements. It will provide you with a snapshot of your net worth. You need a starting point. This financial tool will list out all assets (what you own) and list out all liabilities (what you owe). The difference between your assets and liabilities is your net worth. Just like looking in the mirror, to better understand your spending habits, this is not always easy and may not paint a great picture. For me, this was one of my driving factors for beginning this journey. Looking at where I was and where I wanted to be as well as the path we were on at that time, was not glamorous nor was it a path that would lead me in a good financial direction.

Lesson 1: Know Your Starting Point

Don't be intimidated by a number. I'm serious about that. I know some of you may feel a little overwhelmed when you look at the numbers on the balance sheet, especially if you are like me and are showing a negative number. I felt like I had been punched in the gut when I saw that we had a negative net worth of $8,000. At 23, married with two good careers, I was taken aback, to say the least. I've told you I am competitive and hate to fail, so that number became a challenge. I had already failed at lifeguarding, even though I thought I was pretty athletic, and now I was failing the CPA exams despite studying nonstop, so I certainly was not going to fail financially. No matter how young or old you are and no matter what this number looks like, you can become financially successful if you follow the right steps.

This is a starting point in numbers. It was the place where I thought through my goals. The balance sheet provides that answer. It is different from a budget, which is something you will create in Chapter 4. Always go back to the balance sheet to track your progress toward your goals. You will create your own balance sheet after reading through Lesson 4 in this chapter.

Lesson 2: Evaluate Your Debt and Focus on Your Goals

Another thing during this process that your balance sheet will reflect is your debt, not only in dollars, but also in things, tangibles. This also gave us pause. Certainly we had to have cars, a bed, a house, and Erin would advocate for needing the engagement and wedding ring. But what about all of the other stuff we had bought? We started having real conversations about all of the noise and clutter that we, along with others in general, allowed ourselves to buy. Being the methodical and routine guy that I am, I really don't like all of the stuff. In fact, the kind of systematic person that I am, the less I have and the less I have to worry about, the better and more at peace I feel. That's not to say I live a totally austere life, but I see no value in having things that are bigger, "better," or more ostentatious as a means of status. That is insignificant to me and actually counters the analytical part of my DNA. So in tracking our money, or more precisely, our debt, it also made us evaluate our belief system and ultimately our goals.

Our goals, we realized, were not tied to material objects that are inconsequential and hold no importance or relevance to our lives or to our happiness. You may totally deviate from me on this point. You might also find, like us, that people often get caught up in consumerism. Yet, looking back, especially as glaring as it was on the balance sheet, we knew that all of the stuff we had bought is nothing more than stuff and all too quickly discarded because it actually holds little value and meaning. Eventually it is thrown overboard to lighten the load—usually for more stuff.

We didn't want to continue along that same path. Of course, there are certain things people need, such as a car. But what type of car and how much debt to incur for that car is the point. Evaluate that for yourself. We did that. You may even have dreams such as saving for your children's college, traveling the world, or early retirement. Everyone's goals are different. The key is to ensure the goals you set are the goals that you want and not what others have made you believe you want. We made many trips to consignment shops selling off all unnecessary things. I found it quite liberating. Of course, I would, right! Actually, I am a pretty simple guy with modest tastes.

Concurrently, we halted all spending of any additional things. Having those candid and intimate conversations not only helped us track our spending, but it also provided the beginnings of earnest conversations about our lifelong aspirations. Our goals are certainly different from yours. There should not be judgment about another's goals and dreams, nor should there be judgment about another's lifestyle.

Unfortunately for us, this was not the case. We had challenged the status quo, for us only, but others took it as a personal affront to their lifestyles. Honestly, we didn't care what others did or how they spent their money. I was happy to help with others' personal finances, but we didn't interfere. Regardless, we were on a mission, an aggressive one, to achieve our goals and to pay off all of our debt.

I am not going to tell you that this path is going to be easy or without consequence or sacrifice. It was very frustrating for us. We felt like we were not always making the strides that we wanted to make. We knew our endeavor was ambitious and that our timeline was a bit crazy, but it was doable on paper. The spreadsheets clearly showed us we could meet our goals and how quickly we could achieve that. But patience often has to prevail. At the same time that all of this was unfolding, I was still studying every free moment I could find for the CPA exams, taking them, not always passing them, which irked me, and working crazy long hours auditing for Deloitte. Sometimes it was overwhelming, but we always kept the goal in mind. You will have to do the same thing. You have to know where you are and where you want to go. Track every dollar. Track your spending and keep your sights on your financial success. It will be worth it.

> **Budgeting Rule of Thumb: Should you pay off debt or invest? My rule is to do whatever lets you sleep at night.**

Lesson 3: The Breakdown of the Balance Sheet in Steps

In order to create your balance sheet, you need to list all your assets and your liabilities to see where you are. Then you can set specific goals that you want to reach, such as paying off debt or investing your money. For those of you who are trying to figure out which to do first, pay off debt first or invest, I have a framework video on YouTube that explains how to decide which to do first or if doing both at the same time makes sense. I have added a link to that video in the Resources chapter at the end of the book. For those with debt, how much free cash flow goes toward debt versus investing usually comes down to a hybrid decision.

While doing this, it is important to figure out any assets that you may need in order to reach your goals that you currently do not have. Remember to utilize the assets you currently have as your initial starting point. You also may need to remove some assets if they do not align with your new goals.

You will use a compound interest calculator for investing goals or an amortization calculator for debt payoff goals. In Chapter 4, you will learn how to calculate your debt payoff goals in more detail. Simplistically, you need to calculate your free cash flow from the budget. This will be completed in future steps and you will tie it back to the balance sheet to help you track and plan your path toward your goals.

For debt payoff goals, calculate free cash flow (or the available amount of cash after all of your expenses have been paid) from the budget you will establish. You will learn more about creating budgets in Chapter 4 and also learn to run an amortization schedule for each liability listed.

For investing goals, you will need to use a compound interest calculator to help with this. You will find a free one at the following site: https://www.investor.gov/financial-tools-calculators/calcu lators/compound-interest-calculator. A 7–8% return assumption is what you can use, following my guidance, but you need to bear in mind that even with that, nothing is guaranteed. Add your free cash flow which you calculated from your budget to the "monthly contribution amount" and fill in the number of years you want till you reach your goal. Then click "Calculate." This will provide your estimated investment balance in the number of years that you selected.

Action Plan: Create Your Own Balance Sheet: Assets and Liabilities

To begin, your balance sheet does not need to be anything fancy. Keep it simple, which I believe is one of the keys to success. Bruce Lee is noted for saying "Simplicity is the key to brilliance," which I think aptly applies here.

Step #1: For your balance sheet, download a template online or use a Google or Excel spreadsheet. If you are a paper and pencil kind of person and/or don't care to use the computer, you can also simply list the balances of all of your assets and then list the balances of all of your liabilities.

Step #2: You need to list all of your assets and also list all of your liabilities. I use an Excel spreadsheet for mine and also put a hyperlink next to each asset and liability. The hyperlink goes to my various online accounts for each asset and liability balance. Doing this allows me to quickly and easily find that balance when I update the balance sheet which I do quarterly. It helps streamline things. If it is a liability, I also list the annual percentage rate or the APR. The annual percentage rate is the yearly rate you are charged for a loan—such as your mortgage, student loans, or car—or that you earn on an investment. Listing the APR allows me to quickly see glaring holes. Completing your balance sheet is usually fairly simple. You will simply list all values of the assets you own and liabilities you owe at a point in time. For example, you may have an individual retirement account (IRA) you opened a few years back that you contribute to or even a 401(k) sitting out there at a company you used to work for. If you have an old 401(k), you may want to consider rolling that over to an IRA. I have included a link in the Resources to a free service that will help you do that. Further, if you own assets that have debt attached to them, such as a car or a home, the asset value is the asset if it was sold today. Unless this asset is fully paid off, it will also have an associated liability value, or the outstanding amount owed. The difference between the asset value and the liability value rolls into the net worth calculation. An example is my home. Our house is currently worth $505,000, and we have a $0 liability. So the asset value is $505,000, and the liability value is $0.00. However, if we had a $300,000 mortgage on our house, our asset would still be $505,000, the liability would be listed as $300,000, which would add $205,000 to our net worth. You simply have to subtract the $300,000, the liability, from the $505,000, the asset, to get the net worth. Assets include cash on hand, savings, investments, tangibles such as the value of the car that is owned (not leased), the value of your home that you own after paying off the debt, etc. You can follow the example below for help.

Step #3: Subtract what you owe, your liabilities, from what you own, your assets, and you will have your **net worth**.

Figure 3.1 is a balance sheet template you can use and a downloadable version is in the Resources. It will help you create your own balance sheet. Additionally, you may not need all of the categories, so you will simply disregard what does not pertain to you at this time.

(continued)

(continued)

The (insert last name)'s Balance Sheet As of X/XX/XXXX		
Assets:		
Cash	**Balance**	**Location**
Cash - Checking	-	PNC Bank
Cash - Savings	-	
Cash - Business Bank	-	
Total Cash	-	Rx
Non-Retirement	**Balance**	**Location**
Taxable Brokerage Account	-	Vanguard
Total Taxable Brokerage	-	Rx
Retirement	**Balance**	**Location**
Roth IRA - Jake	-	Fidelity
401k - Jake	-	
Roth IRA - Kara	-	
401k - Kara	-	
ESOP - Kara	-	
Pension Plan - Jake	-	
Total Retirement	-	Rx
Vehicles	**Balance**	**Location**
Car #1	-	Citizens Bank
Car #2	-	
Total Vehicles	-	Rx
Real Estate	**Balance**	**Location**
Rental	-	Chase Bank
Real Estate - Lot	-	
Real Estate - personal residence	-	
Total Real Estate	-	Rx
Total Assets:		Rx
Liabilities:		
Credit Cards	**Balance**	**Location**
CC #1	-	Discover
CC #2	-	
Total Credit Cards	-	Rx
Student Loans	**Balance**	**Location**
Student Loan #1 - Jake	-	PNC
Student Loan #2 - Jake	-	
Student Loan #1 - Kara	-	
Student Loan #2 - Kara	-	
Total Student Loans	-	Rx
Medical Debt	**Balance**	**Location**
X-ray exam	-	PNC
Total Medical Debt	-	Rx
Vehicles	**Balance**	**Location**
Car #1	-	Citizens Bank
Car #2	-	
Total Vehicles	-	Rx
Real Estate	**Balance**	**Location**
Rental	-	PNC
Real Estate - Lot	-	
Real Estate - personal residence	-	
Total Real Estate	-	Rx
Total Liabilities	$ -	Rx
Net worth:		Rx

Figure 3.1 Balance sheet template.

Budgeting Rule of Thumb: It is time to replace your car when maintenance costs are more than the car itself. If you start getting to that point, budget accordingly.

Lesson 4: Understanding Your Net Worth

Now that you have listed your assets and liabilities on the balance sheet, you have a look at your current net worth. It is simple math. Remember that the goal of the balance sheet is to look at where you are at any point in time, so you know your starting point. These are your asset and liability balances on the "as of" that particular date.

You want to increase your net worth, so you have to know what that starting place is, and you need to revisit it and update it with some regularity. I suggest updating your balance sheet quarterly. This is best practice and is a great way to keep track of your wealth-building progress. You can use a basic fiscal cycle (12 months) and update it on March 31, June 30, September 30, and December 31. Of course, you can do it more often, monthly, for example, but keep in mind that the purpose of the balance sheet is to track your goals and to make sure you are trending upward. I don't advise getting caught up in spending more time than on a quarterly basis updating your balance sheet. Just make sure you have a starting point to know what your current net worth is.

When I first completed our balance sheet and discovered that our net worth was a negative $8,000, I was about 23 years old. Needless to say, I was not looking at anything good, just rather ugly to me and a bit daunting. One thing I want to emphasize, however, is that while it is a number showing your net worth, it does not mean you can't change things from the negative to the positive. It was unsettling to me because I thought or had fooled myself into thinking that I was doing fairly well. I had a house, cars, and a career. The balance sheet was key to making me look at my net worth—or lack thereof. Pause here to see just what your numbers show for your net worth.

Own your net worth. This is your beginning. Good or bad, it is your starting point. The good news is that it will only improve from this point provided you put in the time and effort. For me, that negative $8,000 is seared into my brain. I will never forget it.

I save every quarterly balance sheet in a folder by year, so I can look back at every quarter for every year. This is inspiring. You will realize how much financial progress you are actually making.

Understanding my net worth also gave me the opportunity to evaluate not only my current financial situation, but it also made me assess my current life situation. At this time, as I mentioned, I was studying for the CPA exam while also working long, monotonous hours at Deloitte as an auditor. The position often took me away from home. Being newly married, I didn't really like that. Looking down the road of life, I knew that if I stayed on that path, my lifestyle was not going to change from the long hours away nor was it going to change financially in the foreseeable future. I didn't want to continue on that path; I knew I wanted something more out of life, not just financially

It is important to be realistic. But in being so, it also means, at times, things have to be held off until the right time. Here is where the organizational component comes into play.

My wife and I had big dreams and high aspirations, yet we knew that we needed to do certain things in a certain order to get to where we wanted to be some day. At the same time, we did not want some day to be so far in the future that we couldn't live the life we wanted. For a while we felt like we were living in limbo and were just going through the motions.

I continued to study for the CPA exams. Even that proved to be futile. I was spending all of my time and effort working and studying, and I didn't even pass the CPA exams the first few times. I tried to keep in perspective what I knew about the Uniform CPA Exam pass/fail rate, which is traditionally around 50%. This even varies by the quarter and the individual section. So I knew the exam was not supposed to be easy, but I didn't like failing. Remember my story of failing my lifeguard training? This was exponentially worse although that failure still stings a bit—all over doing the incorrect kick! Failing the exams only made me more resolute about passing. Looking back, those situations, frustrations, and failures were all important in helping us on our journey. So do not be afraid of failure. We learn so many valuable lessons from it.

Reflecting on our lives at that time, we "appeared" to be such a normal couple. We had accumulated all of the things that are so much a part of regular life, which also means amassing so much "regular" debt—or so we thought. We had a car loan, a student loan, an engagement and wedding ring loan, and a mortgage. It all seems normal, right? But remember what we discussed in Chapter 2, I refused to buy into the hype that those debts are normal. We knew, looking at the balance sheet and realizing that we actually had a negative net worth, that we needed to make drastic changes in our finances and in our lives. That is what began our conversations that ultimately led us to be able to set goals and to aggressively attack them. You will need to have that same conversation. Do you like what you see on the balance sheet? If not, now is the time to make those changes. You can do it, if I can do it.

Action Plan: Your Net Worth

Step #1: Write down your net worth. It is your beginning.
Step #2: Going forward, save your quarterly balance sheet for tracking. Use them for inspiration and motivation.
Step #3: Update your balance sheet quarterly.

Chapter 4
Craft a Plan: Create Your Budget

Lesson 1: The Importance of Crafting Your Plan

It's a little embarrassing to admit that I did not have all the answers nor didn't make any mistakes at the beginning of my journey. I want you to learn from my mistakes and have an easier time crafting a plan that will lead you to financial freedom and success. I am usually methodical and systematic, which I was in this case as well, but my first big mistake was beginning with a budget rather than setting everything up on a balance sheet. I'll get back to that in a moment, but I want to give you the backstory.

While I was working with my father-in-law, who was helping me build a brick porch on the back of my house, we were discussing loans and finances in general. Like always, I was asking a million questions—shocker! Mostly I was interested in his financial philosophy and how he was able to pay off his debts. Our discussion was also about credit and credit cards. His focus is and has been to only pay for things when he has the money. For example, he was talking about only doing things such as renovations to a house like the porch we were building on my house only when the person actually has the money available to do it rather than borrowing money for it. In other words, we discussed being frugal. This is something I saw again and again with him. His advice to me, as we were floating concrete and laying up brick piers, which is not easy work, to say the least, made sense and really gave me perspective on paying off debt. I knew I couldn't spend myself out of debt. That night, after we finished a long day constructing the porch, I paid off one of my debts, which was the loan for the bed. It was the beginning. While small, it was a start and it was liberating. My point is, don't be afraid to begin with small steps. Everything helps and moves you in the right direction.

Now back to the mistakes and my path that I don't want you to take. I mistakenly began my financial journey with a budget rather than starting with a balance sheet. My organizational framework was not correct. That is why I wanted you to set up a balance sheet first. You have to set that up so you have the starting point from which you can see your growth and can watch yourself trend upward. It is all about *tracking your money*. Using a balance sheet to assess where you are financially at this point in time is key. From there, you will be able to leverage the budget. You can allocate cash flow on the budget to the financial goals that you have listed on the balance sheet. You can refer back to Chapter 3 regarding this.

But my mistake at first was that I concentrated on the budget, thinking that was the main thing that would keep us on track of paying off our bills and getting out of debt. Don't be like me and fall short by missing key steps that will be the framework to your success. Both the balance sheet and budget are important, but they need to be completed in steps so you can best utilize their importance. After crafting your balance sheet, you will create your budget.

Keep in mind the purpose of the budget. A budget is not to restrict you but rather to give you control over your money, as it is a detailed written plan that helps track your money. It can also bring you some clarity and peace of mind in knowing where you are with your spending and how your spending habits can bring you to your financial goals. A notable quote about budgets by Jacob "Jack" Joseph Lew, former U.S. Secretary of the Treasury is, "The budget is not just a collection of numbers, but an expression of our values and aspirations" (Longley, 2019). Taking time to carefully create your budget will give you clarity about your values.

To create our budget, I began with our previous three months of expenses as my way of looking back and creating a starting point—the steps you took in Chapter 2. I really should have started with the balance sheet. Unfortunately, I didn't. But what I did learn through our budget was that we had an additional cash flow of $1,000 per month. We didn't fully realize this until I put everything in the budget. Remember that the budget allows you to control your financial life. Once we saw this in black and white, though, we immediately began applying that amount to my student loans; Erin didn't have any so we aggressively went after my loans.

Budgeting Rule of Thumb: For student loans, your starting salary should be greater than the total debt you take on.

So with the balance sheet, we had a start. However, from my background in accounting and taking everything into account as an auditor of big financially sound companies, I knew the budget and balance sheet were only a part of the true picture and that there was one more key missing ingredient: the amortization schedule, which is needed to accurately complete the financial framework. I continued to draw on my education and training from my professional career as a CPA (I eventually and thankfully passed the exam) to help set up a financial framework.

Since I was in budget mode, however, I set up a zero-based budget which I continue to use today. Zero-based budgeting simply means that every dollar is accounted for. In other words, you earmark or give a classification for all of the money coming in and going out. Think about this. Every dollar coming in has a home or place to go. You do this for every single dollar until you get to zero dollars. You may not get to zero in the very beginning, and that is okay. You may also find when creating your own budget that you have extra money that you can reallocate to other categories such as paying off a debt or putting money toward savings. But you may also discover that you are over-spending. This can be equally important because now you can figure out how to live within your income and where to cut.

For my zero-based budget, I noted our fixed income, which was my income from Deloitte and Erin's income, and added in our vari-able income, which was what we were collecting from various side hustles. From there, I subtracted all of our fixed and variable expenses such as our mortgage payment, which were the same each month (fixed) to our food, which could vary monthly (variable). I also sub-tracted all of our one-time expenses such as our wedding. Savings and investments are also accounted for in the budget. We will discuss this more in depth in Chapter 6 when we delve into growing your money.

Budgeting Rule of Thumb: For budgeting purposes, in order to know how to pay for home maintenance, gen-erally you should set aside 1% of the home's value every year.

Action Plan: Create Your Zero-Based Budget

Now it is your turn. At this time, you need to create your budget, which is the second step in the framework. At Budgetdog Academy, I focus on zero-based budgeting and what I recom-mend for all those with whom I work.

Step #1: Begin by referencing your three-month lookback analy-sis discussed in Chapter 2 from **Action Plan: Three-Month Lookback Analysis**. This will be your starting point to see where you currently stand.

Step #2: List all of the following: Fixed Income (salary), Varied Income (commission, bonuses, extra money from side hustles), Fixed Expenses (mortgage or rent, car payment, utilities, etc.), Variable Expenses (clothing, groceries, gas, etc.), One-Time Expenses (wedding, vacation, new car), and monthly contributions to Savings and Investments (Roth IRA, Sinking Fund, 529 College Savings Plan, etc.).

Step #3: Add your Fixed Income and Variable Income (if applicable).

Step #4: From that amount, subtract ALL of your expenses (Fixed, Variable, One-Time, and Savings/Investments). Do not forget to include things such as insurance that you may only pay quarterly or semiannually.

Step #5: This difference between your Income and Expenses, Savings, and Investments SHOULD be zero. As stated above, if you do not get to zero in the very beginning, that is okay. The goal is to get you there. Here are things to consider. Having a surplus is actually a good problem to have. It shows that your money in the past has been used inefficiently and is likely sitting in cash with no particular goal. You can now allocate that surplus to best meet your personal goals such as paying down debts or putting it into investments. On the other hand, if you have a deficit, that is an opportunity to improve. You can do that by increasing your income or by being more intentional with your spending, thus making sure you don't overspend, causing a deficit. Seeing a deficit when you begin can be emotional but remember that zero-based budgeting is simple addition and subtraction. Do not let this overwhelm you or prevent you from improving.

Step #6: From there, you will actively make decisions to redirect your spending moving forward to the goals that you have, such as paying down debt, increasing investments, or spending on leisure. Saying you will eliminate eating out yet make no actual change to your daily life is not going to be a good solution. Benjamin Franklin said, "If you fail to plan, you are planning to fail!" (Goodreads, n.d.). So stop here and make a plan.

Figuring out what you are comfortable with to spend every month on eating out is where you begin. Let's say that amount is $300 per month. That means you have $75 per week. If your average meal is $25, you know you can reasonably eat out three times during the week. If you know Wednesday nights are late nights at the office and you plan to pick up dinner on Wednesday nights, that is perfect. Most of your budgeting will come down to planning effectively *before* life happens.

The initial setup will take a bit of time, but you will eventually only spend about half an hour each month subsequently. Since our system is already set up, my wife and I personally do two 10-minute check-ins per month. We will track our spending halfway through the month to ensure we are on track and at the end of the month to ensure we meet our goals. If you have the full Budgetdog system in place, this should be easy. You can create your budget on an Excel spreadsheet or by using a hard copy. Personally I like Excel, using my personal Budgetdog system that all of my students use in Budgetdog Academy, but you can also use Mint, YNAB, or Rocket Money.

This next step is for you to analyze where you are. If you find there is extra money that you didn't realize before going through this process of creating a budget, make sure you make a plan where to apply that money. It is imperative that you find a home for every dollar when you are doing zero-based budgeting. Extra money can be applied to debt if you have any, to savings, or to investing. Just ensure that you account for it and don't waste it.

Figure 4.1 is an example of a budget that you can follow using your income and expenses.

Budgeting Rule of Thumb: When creating your budget, keep in mind that your emergency fund should be three to six months of expenses.

JANUARY BUDGET			
Expense Item	Actual	Budget	Difference
Mortgage	1,015	1,015	-
Homeowner's Insurance	52	52	-
Phone	75	75	-
Automobile Insurance	70	70	-
Gym	32	32	-
Internet/TV	81	81	-
Electric	74	74	-
Dogs	404	404	-
Trash Service	26	26	-
Retirement Investing	350	350	-
Non-Retirement Investing	120	120	-
Water	87	85	(2)
Duke Gas	56	53	(3)
Gas for Car	37	47	10
Food	650	680	30
Clothing	100	50	(50)
Wedding Sinking Fund	1,000	1,000	-
New Car Sinking Fund	500	500	-
Miscellaneous	350	402	52
Total Per Month	5,079	5,116	37

Figure 4.1   Budget example.

When I was crafting our plan and trying to track our money, again making some mistakes and feeling a bit frazzled, especially after seeing that we had money on paper that we were not throwing at debt, I began pacing around my living room like a madman. I was on a mission. Again, I was on a journey, but we, together, were not on the same page. Getting Erin on board took some time, effort, and cajoling, to say the least. She was already pretty frugal and had not amassed real debt other than our mortgage, so in her eyes, things were not too bad. The next step was REALLY getting Erin to be as passionate about the plan and the spreadsheets, well, maybe not all of the spreadsheets, but at least as fired up about the plan as me. While I couldn't get her to buy into everything and she was distancing herself from the mountains of spreadsheets that I was creating, I did make some changes that helped enormously overall that she was willing to do. Lesson 2 are things I would suggest to make sure you and your partner are in agreement.

Lesson 2: Organizational Tips for Tracking Your Money

Being organized and systematic are key components of any plan and are areas where I cannot emphasize enough the importance of how it will help you become successful on this journey. Each person will find things that work for himself or herself. Some of us are more organized with things than others. I am, by nature, very systematic, and these are things that have worked for me as well as many of my Budgetdog Academy students. It is important to implement what will actually work for you.

One key thing, an organizational tip, that I did and would highly recommend for simplicity reasons is to consolidate all bank accounts into one joint bank account. Keeping track of one bank account will take you less time and will be easier to manage than multiple accounts. Yes, it may take some time to get things consolidated if your paycheck or paychecks are automatically going into different accounts, but it is usually a fairly quick fix. Make the time to get everything rolled into one bank account.

A second thing I did which I 100% think is key to crafting a good financial plan is to automate everything you can. Turn on automation to pay all of your bills, your investments, your mortgage, your savings, and any debts that you are paying down. Not only will this simplify things for you, but it will also create consistency. Since you aren't thinking about having to pay the mortgage, for example, it is just being paid on a consistent basis.

People are not, by nature, consistent. Some of us are even less consistent than others. I write down everything to book out the time or to do things that I have to or want to do such as "go to the gym at 8:00," or reminders to fill up my 25-ounce water bottle five times a day. If I don't "automate" those things, I won't consistently do them.

Paying bills, putting money into a savings account, and putting money into investments are the same thing. So really make the time to automate everything to establish those consistent habits. We did that and, even today, stay on automation with our investments and with reminders that are necessary to make our lives routine and consistent.

This also means that you won't miss payments, helping your credit rating in the long run. You know the bills are coming out and have to be paid, and you also know what your balance sheet looks like. Therefore, there is no temptation not to pay bills and to use money for different expenses or for spontaneous and/or impulsive spending. As much as I advocate that simplicity is important and fundamental to success, I also firmly believe that consistency is also imperative for success.

Also, think about your expenses such as utilities. Not only can you automate them, but you may be able to move them from the variable expense category to a fixed expense category. You can do this by contacting your utility companies and requesting to be put on budget billing or even billing. Personally, I use budget billing. Budget billing is the trailing of 12 months of usage and then averaging that to provide you with that as your payment. This is a wonderful way to prevent you from having exorbitantly high bills during months when your usage is especially high, such as in extreme cold or hot months. Those surprise bills can wreck a budget. The utility company will contact you if there is going to be a change in that determined monthly amount. The other choice is even billing, which is similar to budget billing. This also spreads the average of your usage from past months. With this type of billing, you have the same bill every month for 11 months. The twelfth month is when the utility company will do an over- or under-analysis for the entire year and adjust your bill accordingly. Either way, budget billing or even billing are methods to move utility expenses from being variable to being fixed, which ultimately helps when you are planning and creating your budget each month.

Another key component to helping craft and plan and stick to the budget that you create is to stop using credit cards. We did that at this early point in our journey. We stopped using our credit cards for everyday spending. I suggest you do this because they are too easy to use. We discontinued using them until we were completely out of debt. This was not difficult for us because we rarely used them anyway and we always paid the balance each month, but we suspended using them because we didn't want to be even remotely tied to anything that insinuated the idea of debt.

People can argue that they like to use credit cards because of the points, saying they use the points for free items, gift cards, flight benefits, etc. Sometimes that is true. For example, if you have a credit card that racks up flight miles and hotel points, and you are the one who gets to utilize those points, then that may be true. But for the masses, the points are overrated and many people quickly get into credit card debt. Remember, the credit card companies bank on you paying only the minimum payment. Not only do they bank on us carrying a balance and thus incurring the interest rate that quickly accumulates, but they know us better than we know ourselves. Remember the psychology of spending that we discussed in Chapter 2? They understand this and make their money by fooling poor "Dan in Wisconsin" who thinks he is getting free money.

However, if you decide to use a credit card, make sure you are tracking your spending, only buying what you have budgeted for that month, and, more importantly, paying the entire balance each month. This is not the amount billed to you but rather the actual amount you have spent. If not, all too quickly, you can find yourself swimming in debt and paying for things that you don't even remember buying.

For us, using a debit card made more sense during our debt paydown. We simply began using the debit card so all of our expenses came out of the checking account immediately. We had to be very deliberate with our spending and cognizant of what was in the account. I can't fully explain what happened psychologically, but we both had a keen awareness that we couldn't just spend randomly. Therefore, before we bought anything, we checked the budget. This definitely helped us remain committed. We already knew what we had budgeted for groceries, for example, so using the debit card was easy and kept our spending more deliberate. Perhaps try switching your credit card for a debit card at this juncture.

Using a joint calendar was another planning method that helped as we planned out our budget a month in advance. Again, it was for simplicity and consistency reasons. You may also find this helpful, especially if you are like many people who are running in different directions and have many things occurring in a month. This isn't for control. Nor was it for one of us to keep tabs on the other. Instead, it was for better communication. It allowed us to more seamlessly plan ahead which ultimately helped me with the budget.

For example, being a young couple, many of our friends were getting engaged and married. Some were even beginning families. This meant we were getting invited to many showers and weddings. It was a time when our friends were still inviting us to things because we weren't being ostracized—yet. That came later. But whether it was family events or things with friends, by having a shared calendar, we could see what was coming up. I could plan accordingly, asking Erin what expenses we would incur for the particular events that were upcoming, such as showers or birthdays. Together, as a married couple, it kept us moving in the same direction; there was no double booking or making plans without checking the calendar.

Overall, for your budget, just like mine, you should spend no more than half an hour each month on it. But that half an hour pays dividends. The budget is an extremely accurate way for you to track your spending, but you don't have to belabor it. Time is money. Your time is valuable, so spending more time than is necessary on your budget each month can be a costly waste of time. Minor adjustments and a look at events and expenses for the upcoming month are all you will have to do once the initial budget is created. Spend time with your initial budget, but that time allotment will diminish over time.

Action Plan: Planning and Organization

Step #1: Read over the organizational tips above and choose one thing this month to implement. This could be automating your

(continued)

(continued)

expenses, switching your utilities to budget or even billing, or using a shared Google calendar, but make it something you can begin right away to help you continue to reach your financial goals.

Step #2: Put that into action for three months to see initial success.

Step #3: Keep working through the list to implement as many as you can to help you stay on track.

Chapter 5

Getting out of Debt:
The Triumph Before
the Real Storm

This chapter begins our discussion about tracking your money. I want you to think of it as the triumph before the real storm. In this chapter I will show you how to be very intentional in order to get out of debt. You will have to brace yourself against futile spending, calculating where all of your money is going, and using all of your extra money to pay off your debts. I will explain amortization schedules, which are helpful not only in tracking your debts and watching them dwindle but also in keeping you fired up about your ultimate goal of being financially independent. Finding extra money, such as doing side jobs and hustles, will also help pay down your debts, and we will suggest some ways to find those opportunities.

Lesson 1: Say No to Spending

What I mean by "say no to spending" is that we were making strides and paying off all our debts, but we were only beginning to embark on our ultimate journey. We had paid off $304,000 in five years, and, on top of that, I quit my 9-to-5 job. There were reasons why I quit Deloitte that I have explained, but the important thing is that I was able to quit because we had paid off our debt and finally had the financial freedom to choose that path.

We continued to say no to futile spending and impulse buying, as we still do today, and to keep our goal in mind. The word "intentionality" always comes to mind when I speak on this topic. It isn't that saying no to things automatically means we aren't "living life," as they say, or not enjoying our life. In fact, the discipline and habits we have created as a result of having a true financial plan make for a much better life! I won't claim I am a Bible reader, but Hebrews 12:11 has always stuck with me: "No discipline seems pleasant at the time, but painful. Later on, however, it produces a harvest of righteousness and peace for those who have been trained by it." Our goal is to be intentional about what matters in life such as family, business, and self-improvement. If an event comes up that does not align with our goals, we do not waste time giving it any attention. We simply say no and align our energy with our current goals. We remain focused on the mission and ignore all else. Your financial statements will be a great tool for guidance and remembering why you are doing what you are doing, but the real change occurs when your habits, behavior, and mindset change to align with what you laid out on your budget and balance sheet. Additionally, you will, like us, continue to do the same things with your balance sheet and budget that you were already doing. Everything was automated and our plan was in full swing. You should be in the same situation at this point. If you are not, go back and follow the steps you skipped.

Lesson 2: Amortization Schedules for Debt Payoff Success

One thing that helped us see progress was the amortization schedules. If you don't have debt, you do not need amortization schedules. You will want to utilize amortization schedules, which simply is the detailed listing of your debts such as student loans, car payments, and mortgages as well as the due date for each loan and the term of the loan. The schedules also include the total loan payment of each loan and the interest rate for each. You can set these up through an online site such as Vertex42 or by working your plan with me at Budgetdog (link provided in Resources). They aren't difficult, and the beautiful thing about amortization schedules is that you can see the progress you are making toward paying off each debt. Figure 5.1 shows an example of an amortization schedule.

Any extra money we had, including the money from selling off our unwanted and unneeded items online and at consignment shops, along with money from side hustles, we threw at the loans and watched the principal payment drop drastically. Being the numbers nerd that I am, I got psyched. I mean really pumped. Even Erin was excited watching the principal amounts go down.

Keep in mind that when you make any extra payments or put any extra money toward your debts, that amount goes directly toward the principal amount. That is why I advise people to pay anything toward that principal amount and to pay as often as you can. Keep at it. You will be happily surprised to see those debts dwindle. We attacked the smallest ones we had by dollar amount, eliminating them one by one. This is called the snowball method. Figure 5.2 is an example of how you would structure your debts using this snowball method. As you can see, you list them in order of dollar amount from least to greatest.

Many financial advisors will advise you to do the same thing, but some will tell you to go after the ones with the highest interest rates. This method is known as the avalanche method. With this method, you simply pay the greatest interest rate debt to the least interest rate debt in order. Figure 5.3 is an example of how you would structure your debts using this avalanche method. As you can see, you list them in order of interest rate from greatest to least.

Deciding to use the snowball method or the avalanche method is an individual situation and preference; it is one that I would want to discuss with you on a personal basis. For most people, deciding

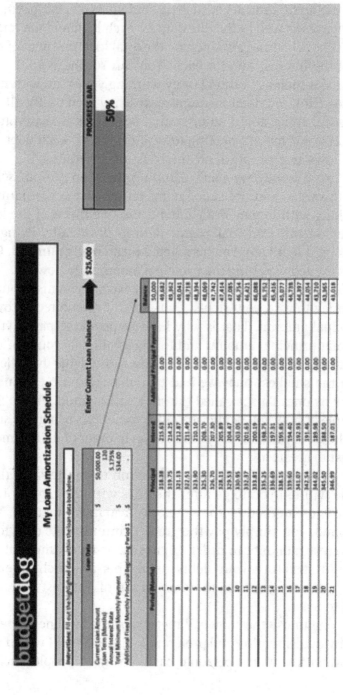

Figure 5.1 Amortization schedule example.

Snowball Method		
Type of Debt	Amount	Interest rate
Credit Card	$ 5,633	23.00%
Car	$ 17,855	4.00%
Student Loan	$ 40,000	5.50%

Figure 5.2 The snowball method example illustrates how to organize your debts by listing debts in order, beginning with those that have the least amount of debt to those with the largest amount of debt.

Avalanche Method		
Type of Debt	Amount	Interest rate
Credit Card	$ 5,633	23.00%
Student Loan	$ 40,000	5.50%
Car	$ 17,855	4.00%

Figure 5.3 The avalanche method attacks debt in order of the interest rate rather than the debt amount.

which method to use often comes down to a hybrid approach, which is the method I most prefer and use.

When deciding which method to use, analysis of the person and the financial situation is key. When I assess my student's situation, for example, I listen to better understand what type of person they are and what would motivate that individual to push through more—the avalanche method or the snowball method. Some people are more emotional so the snowball method works better for them, seeing even a small debt paid off is exciting and motivating, but for those who are more logical, the avalanche method is best. This will usually be the main steps through which I take them, but I also have to consider a few other things such as preferences, balances, and rates. Some people may want to pay off some of their debts, but not other debt. I provide my professional opinion, but it's not my money so ultimately, each person has to decide what is most important. I simply guide my students based on what they want to do or achieve while giving my professional opinion for guidance and support.

Some students do not fall into one specific category in which a pure snowball method or a pure avalanche method would work. For that person, I recommend the hybrid method. For example, let's say one of my students has $70,000 or so of debt and five debts. Of those five debts, one debt is 0% interest and has only $1,000 remaining, but paying that one debt results in a lot of cash flow. I would suggest paying that one particular debt off first before the others. That is a hybrid. From there, we could look at attacking the others using one of the other methods.

Regardless of how you pay off the debt, the amortization schedules are huge in showing you progress. Remember we talked about your net worth and the importance of having a starting place? This is why. During the time we were paying down our debt, I reviewed those amortization schedules like it was my day job. I didn't have to spend time reworking the schedules because they were all set up and basically done. The only time I had to manually change them was when we made additional one-time payments.

Our amortization schedules provided us with the confidence that we were on track to pay off our debts with our original timelines that we planned for. But we were not there yet and had more to accomplish.

Lesson 3: Stay on Track

At this point, your timelines should all be activated and your plan should be coming together. For us, that was very much the case. Things were coming to fruition. You, just like us, will need other pieces of the framework that I will discuss in upcoming chapters, but, overall, we started to see light and to feel successful. You will have that same success if you are following this plan and not skipping any steps. Remember this is a methodical process, so you must take this journey step-by-step. As you do, you will edge closer to the finish line. The important thing to do at this point is to hold firm to the things you have listed on your plan. This will take fortitude and restraint. You have to resist any temptations and fight against all distractions. Keep in mind your money mindset and have a plan for negative cognitions. It is easy to become beguiled into relaxing but resist and keep your goal in mind. Being debt-free and financially independent is so much more important than any item you may think you need. Stay the course. It will be worth it.

I think this is where the plan and the progress we made really taxed our fortitude needed to be successful. We were fully committed, so we knew we could not become complacent. That meant our Fridays and Saturdays were no longer days for going out, spending money, and being reckless. These became days for staying in to work on building up Budgetdog or time committed to side hustles such as working some construction jobs or Erin doing freelance renderings for architects. Sundays were also meal prep days and organizational days for the week. Most people, as we all too quickly found out, didn't understand and see the need for such a lifestyle change and adjustments. It is countercultural. You may be met with resistance from others to go out and spend money, forget about your budget, and live a little. All I can say is to keep your personal goal in mind and let them live as they wish to live.

Mentally we committed to this plan which took us just one year! Think about that. One year of sacrifice to reap such benefits. Let's put this into action for you.

Action Plan: Organize Your Debts

1. **Step #1:** Begin your action plan by listing all of your debts (which are on your balance sheet already). These may include credit card debt, student loans, high interest loans, IRS debt, etc.
2. **Step #2:** Organize your debts so you can begin to attack each debt. You can use the snowball method, avalanche method, or a hybrid method. Remember to contact me directly if you are confused about which method is best for you.

Action Plan: Debt Payoff

1. **Step #1:** Debt-by-debt, you will pay off each one using the method you decided on. Throw any extra money you can at the debts.
2. **Step #2:** I personally automated the additional principal payments at the end of each month. Paying off your debts will also clean up or improve your credit rating.

Action Plan: Stay on Track

I know this is not easy, nor happens overnight, but this will ensure you stay on track. Keep watching the amortization schedules for motivation. Each payment gets you that much closer to your goal. Becoming creative here is the goal. I have a list of potential side hustles for you listed below. Remember a side hustle is NOT usually fun and can be gritty and not so desirable. Doing construction, one of my side hustles, was grueling, hot, and tiring, to say the least. My advice is to keep your WHY in mind. The goal of your side hustle is to bring in any additional income you possibly can as fast as possible to help you fast-track your ultimate goals. Not taking any action is simply flirting with procrastination.

Side Hustle Ideas

Uber/Lyft, Amazon, Rover, Etsy, eBay, Plasma Donation, Affiliate Marketing, Fiverr, Poshmark, Facebook Marketplace, OfferUp, Remote Setting/Closing, and consignment shops.

Part II

Grow Your Money

Chapter 6

Setting the Stage for Your Investments

B y now, you have a good understanding of where you are financially and where you want to be not only financially but also personally, hopefully setting up some pretty awesome and lofty goals. The foundation has been laid. Through the tracking your money steps of my Budgetdog framework, you have created your balance sheet, which has given you a clear picture of your net worth, you have also created your budget, and you are using your amortization schedules. Additionally, you should also have everything consolidated into one bank account and have automated all the payments possible for simplicity and consistency reasons.

At this time, not only do you have a good foundation, but you should also be feeling a bit more at ease, knowing that you are on a good trajectory for success. You are tracking your money and are fully aware where every dollar is going. Continue to use a zero-based budget to help you track every dollar. Setting up this framework first is really key. You are creating good habits that will help your continued success so don't skip any of the steps as discussed up to this point. These good habits of simplicity and consistency will bleed over into other aspects of your life, helping you become much more aware and disciplined, and, thus, exponentially improving many areas of your life.

Now that you are here, having firmly created this solid framework, it is time to really **grow your money**. There is no mystery here or secret formula. There are a variety of ways that you can use to grow your money by investing it and there are a variety of places such as the stock market where you can invest. In this chapter, you will learn the basics for investing and keys that can help you become financially independent.

Investing Rule of Thumb: The Rule of 72: This rule is an equation that lets you know how long it will take an investment to double.

72 ÷ [rate of return] = [years it will take initial investment to double]

Example : 72 ÷ 10% = 7.2 years to double an investment

For ease of math, a way to simplify this is to aim at having your investments double every 10 years.

Lesson 1: Compound Interest

A basic and most wonderful principle that applies to investing is compound interest. Albert Einstein clearly understood the mathematical wonder behind compound interest, noting, "Compound interest is the eighth wonder of the world. He who understands it, earns it . . . he who doesn't . . . pays it" (Einstein, n.d.). The idea of compound interest is fairly simple and works on time. The more time you have for your money to grow, the more it will grow exponentially. So, the more time you have in the market, the more your money will grow. Simplistically, your money grows faster because it is compounding, so the interest on your money gets calculated over time as well as the principal, so it is interest on the interest as well as the principal. It continues to snowball, growing bigger and bigger over time.

For ease of math, Figure 6.1 shows a simple scenario comparing simple interest compared to compound interest. With simple interest, all you get is interest on the principal. So if you have $1,000 and you are getting 10% interest, your principal always stays the same. After three years, you will only have $1,300. Let's break that down year by year for a better understanding.

The first year, your interest of 10% on the $1,000 would give you $100 for a total of $1,100. The second year, the 10% is still only on that $1,000.00 principal, so you would now have $1,200, having earned another $100 in interest. Likewise, the third year, getting only interest on the principal, you would have a total of $1,300. With compound interest, however, your interest and principal will change. Keeping the same amounts, what happens is that after three years, instead of $1,300, you will actually have $1,331. The reason is because you have $1,100 after the first year, and the 10% interest is applied to the $1,100 over the second year, which compounds to $1,210 after the second year, then to $1,331 after the third year ($1,210 x 10%) (Figures 6.2, 6.3, and 6.4).

While that does not seem very dramatic, the difference only being $31 in this example, imagine what that could be with a bigger starting amount than $1,000 and a longer time span than three years. Think in

Simple Interest Calculator

Balance	Principal	Term	Rate
Principal	$1,000		
Interest rate	10 % per year		
Term	3 years		
Calculate ▶ Clear			

Results

End Balance: $1,300.00
Total Interest: $300.00

Calculation steps:
Total Interest = $1000 × 10% × 3
= $300.00
End Balance = $1000 + $300.00
= $1,300.00

Figure 6.1 Simple interest calculator calculation.

Step 1: Initial Investment

Initial Investment *
Amount of money that you have available to invest initially.

$1,000

Step 2: Contribute

Monthly Contribution
Amount that you plan to add to the principal every month, or a negative number for the amount that you plan to withdraw every month.

$0

Length of Time in Years *
Length of time, in years, that you plan to save.

1

Step 3: Interest Rate

Estimated Interest Rate *
Your estimated annual interest rate.

10

The Results Are In

In **1** years, you will have **$1,100.00**

Figure 6.2 Simple interest and how it works over a three-year span which is striking compared to the same amount of money with compound interest.

terms of $1 million. The first year you would have $1,100,000. The second year, due to compound interest, it would be $1,210,000. But after 10 years, you would have $2,593,742 because you amass money on the interest and on the principal with compound interest compared to simple interest. Remember, with simple interest, the principal always stays the same. After 10 years, with simple interest, your principal is still only $1,000, so you are only gaining interest on that amount. It will never grow exponentially.

Let's look at an example to help further illustrate this concept. In Figure 6.5, we have Oscar and Denise. Oscar invests $1,000 per month from ages 18 to 30 and never invests again after age 30,

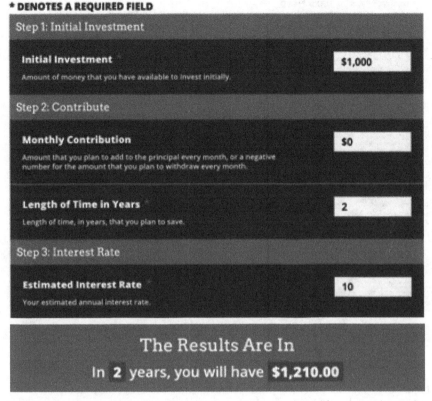

Figure 6.3 The amount of interest the same investment would make with simple interest at the end of year 2.

letting that principle compound going forward. Denise decides to wait to invest until she is 30 years old. She invests $1,000 per month every month from age 30 until age 60.

During this total period (age 18–60), Oscar contributed $144,000 in total during the initial 12 years he invested. Denise, however, contributed $360,000 to her investments from age 30 to age 60. It looks like Denise was the wise one as she invested more and longer. But wait!

At age 60, Oscar actually has $4,477,715 (Figure 6.6), and Denise only has $1,973,928 (Figure 6.7). How? It comes down to time.

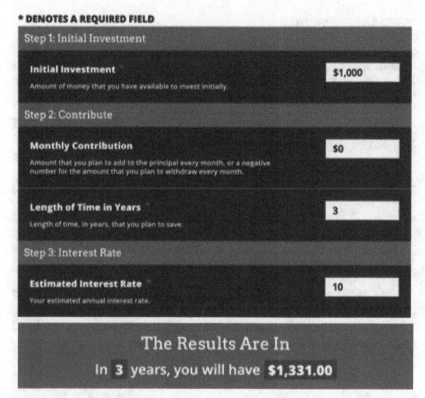

Figure 6.4 At the end of the third year with simple interest, the amount of interest is indicated.

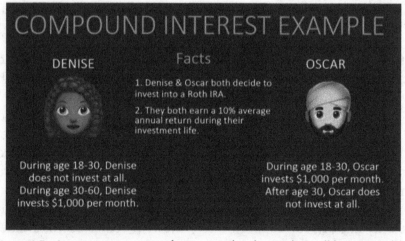

Figure 6.5 In comparison to simple interest, this shows what will happen with compound interest.

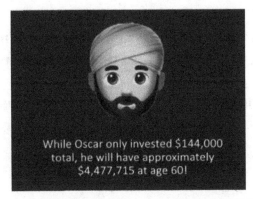

Figure 6.6 Oscar's contributions have time on his side, thus eliciting a larger amount overall.

Figure 6.7 Even though it seems Denise contributed more than Oscar during ages 18–60, time was not on her side. Therefore, her total amount is far less than Oscar's.

While Denise actually contributed $216,000 more than Oscar during ages 18–60, Oscar had more time on his side for compound interest to work its magic.

It is impossible to beat time. That is why it is imperative to start NOW. There is no time to wait. It gets more expensive the longer you wait or at least more costly.

Investing Rule of Thumb: In order to be a millionaire by age 60, you need to invest the following amounts:

Starting age	Investment per month $
20	290
30	670
40	1,700
50	5,500

Lesson 2: Investing 101: Understanding Stock Market Basics

You are in investor mode, wanting to grow your money and accumulate wealth, so let's start discussing the stock market and some of the basics of investing. I won't use my bee-killing company as an example to help explain the market basics because it didn't last very long nor yield much of a return. Instead, especially since I like enterprise and entrepreneurship, I will use an example of a kid, Charlie, and his lawn care business.

When Charlie decided to open his first lawn care business in his neighborhood, he was just 16 years old. For him to begin operating the business, Charlie had to assess what the business needed. He concluded that he would need approximately $1,000 total in order to begin his lawn care business. His current bank account balance showed just $500 cash, so he knew that he would need to raise $500 from friends in his neighborhood. Charlie brainstormed two ways to do this: through issuing stocks and bonds. He wanted to retain as much ownership as possible of his business, but he also wanted to provide as much incentive as he could so that his friends would want to invest in his business.

For the first $250, Charlie decided to offer ownership, or stock, to all his friends who were interested in the exchange for cash.

He decided to have an Initial Public Offering, or an IPO. An IPO is the process of offering shares, or stock of a private corporation to the general public, Charlie's friends, in this example.

For the other $250, Charlie decided to allow some of his friends to lend him $250, which is called a bond. He promised these friends that he would return the full $250 amount plus 5% interest within one year.

Four of Charlie's friends wanted to become part of his business. Nick and Karlie wanted to become owners within the business, so each bought one share of stock in Charlie's lawn care business for $125 per share. Jerry and Niko decided they would rather be guaranteed their money back with a small return. Therefore, they each decided to lend Charlie $125 for a company-issued bond.

Charlie opened for business and the profits began pouring in. In the first year alone, Charlie amassed $10,000 in sales. The shareholders, Nick and Karlie, were ecstatic about Charlie's profits, and the bondholders, Jerry and Niko, were happy that they would be repaid their money along with the earned 5% interest.

As promised, Charlie paid Jerry and Niko, his two bondholders, their $125 plus 5% interest ($125 + $6.25 = $131.25).

Since Charlie's profits rose much faster than originally anticipated, the word of Charlie's lawn care business spread to other kids in the neighborhood. The demand for Charlie's stock was so high that the stock price increased to $250 from $125 in one year. At this point, Charlie had to make his stock cheaper so that more of his friends were actually able to afford it. He had a goal to split the share price in half, and the only way he could do that was by doubling the number of shares each shareholder currently owned. Charlie decided to do a two-for-one stock split so more friends would be able to purchase stock in his company. Nick and Karlie now each owned two shares instead of one. Each share was back to just $125 per share instead of $250 per share. They both still had the same amount of ownership within the company, however, there was a redistribution of their capital.

The two-for-one stock split did nothing to fundamentally change the business, but it allowed more friends to invest at a more reasonable price of $125 per share. Other friends in the neighborhood wanted to become part of the business, too. One in particular, Caleb, decided to offer Nick $500 for both shares of stock that he owned in Charlie's lawn care company. Caleb knew that there were only four shares total offered by Charlie, and he also knew Nick owned two of them. Nick couldn't pass up this offer; he sold both of his shares of stock to Caleb for a total of $500. Nick profited $375 ($500 sales price minus the $125 original purchase price) in total.

Unlike Nick, Karlie understood that Charlie's lawn care business was a great company to be a part owner in for the long term, so she did not sell her stock in the business. She believed that Charlie was shrewd, and the demand for cutting grass would never go away.

Charlie also saw the potential of his growing business and decided to expand. He wanted to reinvest all business profits back into his company in the early stages of the business.

In the early stages of a business, a company should reinvest all of their profits back into the business to accelerate growth. But as that company grows and becomes more stable, the company should begin to reward its shareholders by sharing a piece of their profits, or dividends.

As Charlie wanted to copy the blueprint of many great companies that have come before him, Charlie's plan was to eventually have enough savings to pay his shareholders a piece of the pie or dividends. With help from the cash received from the stocks and bonds that Charlie issued, Charlie decided to expand and begin cutting grass in the other neighborhoods close by.

In order to do this, Charlie needed to purchase a shed to store his equipment. There happened to be a shed available in his neighborhood, and he had the option to rent or buy the shed. He decided to purchase the shed from Steve for a fair price of $500. He understood two things. First, his business would be around for a long time, and also that the market he purchased the shed in was going to see big gains in the coming years.

He had many future ideas for this real estate. His options were to retain the shed, rent half of the shed out to his brother for his weed pulling business or completely sell the shed if he found a better location in the future. Since he owned the shed, he had the power to decide as well as the ability to decide when, if ever, to sell.

In order to get back and forth from neighborhood to neighborhood, Charlie also purchased a four-wheeler and a small trailer with some of the profit he received from the business.

Additionally, there were two local gas stations offering the commodities he needed: gas and oil. He set up a meeting with both gas stations to discuss how much gas and oil he would need annually. Bob's Gas Station offered a fixed amount contract of gas and oil for $.05 per gallon cheaper than Tom's Towing and Gas Station. He accepted the contract offer from Bob's Gas Station, and Charlie began to cut grass in multiple neighborhoods.

Charlie continued in business for years. Throughout that time, more and more friends wanted to purchase a piece of his business. He was able to begin providing quarterly dividends to all of his shareholders. Charlie's neighborhood became a real-life representation of the stock market.

This example is simplistic, but this is how easy the markets really are. There are a lot of fancy terms thrown around to make you feel like you cannot participate or need the help of a professional, but that is not the case. If you have a fundamental understanding of the market, you will be able to excel in the financial markets today.

Investment Rule of Thumb: Keep in mind your net worth benchmarks. Compute this by multiplying your age by your gross annual income divided by 10.

Equation : [Age] × [Gross annual income] ÷ 10 = your target net worth

A 30-year-old with a $100k annual salary should be worth $300,000.

$30 \times 100,00 / 10 = \$300,000$ net worth.

Lesson 3: Understanding Types of Asset Classes

One key component in understanding investing is to have an awareness of the different types of assets that investors can buy and sell. There are five main types of asset classes (Figure 6.8): (1) cash and cash equivalents; (2) stocks (equities); (3) bonds (fixed income); (4) real estate; (5) and commodities (real assets). Let's look at the different asset classes for a better understanding of the nuances of each.

Asset Class 1: Cash and Cash Equivalents

We are talking about money in the form of money market accounts, Treasury Bills, Certificates of Deposit (CDs), money orders, notes, coins, and physical paper bills (which can be in liquid funds), savings accounts, and even online wallets. Cash does not increase in value in real terms. If you have a $100 bill today, it will be worth much less in 10 years due to inflation. Cash has a place and a value, but it is not a good investment in and of itself due to inflation, which is approximately 3% annually. Because of that, I usually recommend keeping cash assets to a bare minimum.

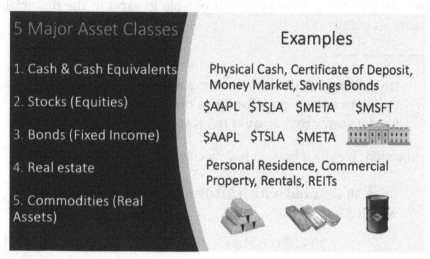

Figure 6.8   The five asset classes.

There are several other key strategies regarding cash that you may want to keep in mind. There are rules that I use for my personal investing. One strategy that I suggest is to have 3–6 months of expenses, your emergency fund, and a savings account, which is a money market account or high-yield savings account like Ally Bank.

Another investing tip regarding cash is to keep 1–2 months of monthly expenses in a checking account, so you can readily pay bills if necessary. Have that accessible for if or when the need should arise.

You can also include in this mix a sinking fund, which is a fund or savings that you periodically set money aside for purchases that you know are upcoming. These are purchases you know you need to buy in the near future and for which you budget. For example, if you know you need to buy a washer and dryer in a year and it is going to cost you $1,800, you will save $150 each month in your sinking fund. At the end of the year, you would have the amount needed for that purchase. Beyond that, all of our cash goes toward investments.

Rule of Thumb for Cash:

1. **Keep 1–2 months of expenses in a checking account.**
2. **Have 3–6 months of expenses in high yield savings account (HYSA) for your emergency fund.**
3. **Set aside relevant money for your sinking fund.**
4. **All other cash should be used toward fast-tracking your goals.**

Asset Class 2: Stocks (Equities)

The next asset class to consider is stocks or equities. Buying a stock or stocks is, in essence, buying a portion of a business or having ownership in the business or company. Likewise, it entitles the stock owner to a portion, whatever amount of stock you purchase, of the business's assets and profits. Units of stock are called shares. Historically, stocks have seen real returns of around 5–7% (but will vary greatly stock to stock).

In the example of Charlie and his lawn care business, Charlie established his IPO at $125 per share. As the company's performance improved, the demand for the company stock went up, ultimately raising the price to $250 per share. The stock price varied with supply and demand. At that point, Charlie decided to go forward with a 2-for-1 stock split. Stock splits are often in the news. It is a simple math equation. If a share price is $1,000 and they do a 5-for-1 stock split, the company will simply divide the current share price of $1,000 by five, to arrive at a new share price of $200. If you are a current investor and own 10 shares of that stock, you now own five times that, or 50 shares of stock. Ultimately, you still own the same amount of stock value. Ten shares times $1,000 is $10,000. 50 shares times $200 is also $10,000. Therefore, you still own the same total amount of equity—$10,000. It is just a redistribution of your equity. Most companies strategically do this so that the stock price is cheaper, which allows more investors to buy the stock. This increases the capital for the company. Fundamentally, the company is the same before and after the stock split. However, the company usually gains traction from the media and that creates hype. In the short term, a stock split can sometimes drive up the stock price from the additional demand from the new announcement.

Going back to our example of Charlie, when the stock split occurred, Nick sold both of his shares and Karlie held onto both of her shares. This is how the real financial markets work. A company that is private will not be able to have public shareholders until the company does what is called an IPO, as discussed above. At this point, the company determines what their share price will be and issues that share price to the public. Investors can now purchase stocks at that given price.

When investors buy shares of a company, their value in that stock can increase through capital appreciation, the increase in share price, or by the dividends that the company will pay their shareholders. When investors speak of their nominal investment returns, they are including capital appreciation and dividends not considering inflation.

Historically, the share price on the date of an IPO will often-times drop right after the stock goes public. Investors will drive up the price and shortly after the IPO, the stock price will drop back down to a more normal price. It happens more times than not. I do not time the market, but it is something to be aware of if you are purchasing individual stock.

Rule of Thumb for Stocks: For retirement, calculate 120 − age = % in stocks. The remainder should go to other assets listed here.

Example : 120 − 60 (person's age) = 60% invested in stocks.

Asset Class 3: Bonds (Fixed Income)

A bond is an instrument of indebtedness of the bond issuer to the holders. The most common types of bonds include municipal bonds and corporate bonds. Bonds can be in mutual funds or in private investing where a person would give a loan to a company or to the government. Historically, bonds have a return of around 1–3% (but will vary greatly bond to bond).

A company will issue debt to investors. As an incentive, the company will pay the investors back the original loan amount plus interest. Bonds are considered a safer investment than stocks as your return is based on the ability of the company to pay.

A company will issue debt to investors like Charlie did selling bonds to Jerry and Niko. As an incentive, the company will pay the investors back the original loan amount plus interest. At the same time, each bond receives a bond rating from a rating service. Companies want to be rated an AAA bond rating. They are able to do so if they can easily meet financial commitments and have the lowest

risk of default. A bond rating is a way to measure the creditwor-
thiness of a bond, which corresponds to the cost of borrowing for
an issuer. Private independent rating services such as Standard &
Poor's (S&P) and Moody's Investors Service evaluate a bond issuer's
financial strength or its ability to pay a bond's principal and interest
in a timely fashion.

As with all assets, the riskier the bond grade, the higher return
that you will potentially receive.

Asset Class 4: Real Estate

This asset class is usually pretty easy to understand as it simply is land
or buildings in which people invest. Personal residence real estate,
like other real estate, shows actual returns that vary by the type of
real estate such as commercial real estate and the current market.

When it comes to real estate, most investors think their only
option is to purchase commercial property like a strip mall, resi-
dential property in which the investor will buy a property and rent
to tenants, and land. Investors pretty quickly conclude whether
this type of investment is suitable for them. However, there is
another type of real estate that many investors don't know about.
This fantastic financial product is called a Real Estate Investment
Trust or REIT.

REITs are companies that own or finance income-producing
real estate across a range of property sectors. These real estate companies must meet several requirements to qualify as REITs. Most
REITs trade on major stock exchanges, and REITs offer a number of
benefits to investors. These financial products are bought and sold
like mutual funds and are a good option for diversifying a financial
portfolio.

Asset Class 5: Commodities

When we discuss commodities, think about things such as products that we, consumers, use. Many times these are natural products
such as agricultural products like wheat and corn. They also include

things such as oil or even gold and silver. Obviously there is a huge difference between corn and gold or wheat and oil. Since commodities differ, so does the return. The rate of return on commodities, overall, is usually on the lower side of the rate of return.

Let's go back to our example about Charlie and his business. Charlie purchased a gas and oil contract from Bob's Gas Station. Stocks and bonds are not physical in nature, but commodities are. Commodities are tangible. This often gives investors a sense of confidence. There is less volatility with commodities and they are usually favored in times of down markets when they are used as a "hedge" or a protection against further losses. Gold, silver, oil, and gas are some of the most popular forms of commodities.

Rule of Thumb for Bonds, Real Estate, and Commodities: Using the equation from the Rule of Thumb for stocks, which is your age subtracted from 120, the remainder of what is not put in stocks should go into bonds, real estate, and/or commodities. The percentage for each of these three depends on the type of investor you are.

Example : $120 - 50 = 70$.

So, 70% goes into stocks, but the other 30% should go into bonds, real estate, and/or commodities.
I have a great video explaining portfolio allocation:
https://www.youtube.com/watch?v=7iglAEju0mM

Lesson 4: Breaking Down Equity Asset Classes

Since you now understand the five major asset classes, let's take this one step further. Just as the term fruit doesn't tell you the exact kind of food you are buying or eating, such as an apple or grapes, stock doesn't tell you the exact kind of investment. A stock is simply ownership in a company. Stocks can be domestic or foreign, small or large, value or growth, etc. Below are the three best-known ways of breaking down each equity asset class.

1. Growth, Value, and Blend Stocks

When it comes to growth, value, and blend stocks, think of growth and value as their own category and blend to be a mix of both. When you think of growth stocks, think of Amazon. This stock is expensive relative to earnings as based on its price to earnings ratio, but the investor believes that the stock price is justified by its high potential in the future. For value stocks, think of CVS or Walgreens. Every town seems to have a CVS or a Walgreens usually on the corner of an intersection. It is essential to the economy, is safe, and is steady. Value stock is a low-priced stock relative to its earnings. There is a lesser downside with owning a stock like this because they are usually more tenured, stable, and mature. So, which type of stock is right for you? None is right or wrong. Some factors to consider as you are developing the right mix for your portfolio are age, risk profile, goals, and timeline. All types of stock can be used to an investor's advantage and benefit if he or she understands them.

2. Location

You guessed it. Location is simply where a company is based.

There are three popular location categories you will often see when analyzing equity options. These include the United States, meaning the actual company is based or located here. Foreign Developed, the second category, refers to companies that are outside of the United States and are in countries that have developed economies and accepted currencies. The last stock option is Foreign Emerging. This references companies that are also outside of the United States, but these companies are in countries that have what is generally considered underdeveloped economies and are considered to be riskier and more volatile or unstable. However, they often yield higher than expected returns. The countries that currently fall under Foreign Emerging include Brazil, Russia, India, and China, or BRIC for short.

3. Market Capitalization

Investors like to use fancy terms like "market capitalization." This simply is the total value of the company stock within the actual stock market. The formula to compute this value is the total number of shares times the share price, which is the way the S&P 500 Index determines its rankings. The S&P 500 Index stands for Standard & Poor's 500 Index. It includes the 50 largest U.S. companies as determined by market capitalization. This makeup of the S&P 500 Index can change over time as companies gain and lose market share.

There are four main market capitalization classifications for companies of which you should be aware for investing purposes: large-cap, mid-cap, small-cap, and micro-cap.

Large-cap or large-market capitalization deals with companies that have a value that exceeds $10 billion. Companies that are in the middle range from about $2 billion up to $10 billion are all in the mid-cap category. For companies with a market value that is less than $2 billion but generally greater than $300 million, their classification is small-cap. Lastly, micro-cap or micro market capitalization companies have a value less than $300 million.

Lesson 5: Diversification

Now that you understand the different types of assets available to you and the way each equity asset class is broken down, it is time to figure out how you, the investor, will decide which investment options are right for you. This is about the time when some people decide to call in a professional, but I warn you that may not be your best option. You are mastering everything there is to know as an investor. As we dive into diversification, remember that less is *usually* more. A portfolio with one to four investments is usually better performing than one with 10 investments.

Understand that there is no *right* way to model your portfolio. Even most of the financial gurus believe in different portfolio models, and they have had great financial success. There is not a one-size-fits-all method, which is why I am presenting you with everything there is to know before creating your own portfolio.

The best place to begin is with a simple rule of thumb for retirement accounts specifically. In order to figure out how much stock and other asset allocation you should have, subtract your age from 120. Some people prefer to use 100 minus your age, but I think that is too conservative. So, if you are 35 years old, 120 – 35 is 85. If you choose to use this as a rule of thumb, you will allocate 85% of your investment dollars in stocks and the remainder between bonds, real estate, and commodities. Again, this is a rule of thumb for retirement account allocation and this amount should be *approximately* how much you have of each asset type.

Some investors may want more stock, some may want more bonds, some will want more real estate, while others may want more commodities. So, what is the perfect blend? One suggestion is to check out the All Weather Portfolio, which is nothing more than an investment portfolio that attempts to perform well almost regardless of economic situations. Like almost anything, this too is subjective. For example, Ray Dalio is a famous American investor who is worth billions (Lazy Portfolio EFT, 2023). According to his famous All Weather portfolio, an investor should invest 55% in bonds, 30% in stocks, and 15% in commodities. Many investors contend having 55% in bonds is too high. However, Dalio's All Weather investment portfolio typically has yielded a little over 7%. That includes minimal drawdowns compared to the market. A drawdown is how much an investment account is down from the peak before it recovers back to the peak. This is temporary and it is considered an "unrealized loss" or paper loss. The only way a "realized loss" occurs is if you proceed to sell the assets at those depressed prices. Another thing an investor needs to consider is the purpose of the asset allocation. In Dalio's example, he is more focused on allocation of risk rather than allocation of capital. Allocation of capital is designed to find the most efficient investment strategy with the goal to maximize profits, whereas allocation of risk (in Dalio's model above) is designed to focus on the risk of each asset class rather than the amount of money in each asset.

Personally, I adhere to the philosophy that portfolio diversification allocation is a six-step process. Here is my advice and my portfolio allocation and management procedure:

1. The first step is to gain an understanding of your risk profile. This allows you to fully understand who you are, not only an investor but as a person. Are you generally a risk-taker or are you more conservative with your money? You have to assess that in order to be able to decide what types of assets you wish to invest in—more conservative ones or riskier ones. For right now, just keep in mind what you think you are, but we will cover this in more detail in Chapter 7, Lesson 6: Risk Profile for Investing.

2. You need to figure out your asset class mix. This is where you will decide if you want stocks and bonds; just stocks; stocks, bonds, commodities, and/or any real estate. The mix is up to you.

3. The third step is the step where you also need to decide how much you want to allocate to growth versus value as well as large-cap versus mid-cap, small-cap, or micro-cap.

4. Here you are deciding whether or not you want to be an active or passive investor. I will tell you that it is very rare to beat the market. In fact, on average, only about 8% of active mutual fund managers beat the market each year and of that 8%, not many do it the next year. Those are the most educated financial minds in the world and 92% lose. It is your decision ultimately how active or passive you want to be; I am a passive investor.

5. This is a key step. As an investor, you need to understand all of the investment fees involved. I will discuss this in more depth in Chapter 7, Lesson 3: Fees: What They Are and Why They Matter So Much.

6. This is your last step and it is critical. Leave your portfolio alone. Seriously. You should review and rebalance it at least annually, but leave it alone other than that. Give the investment choices you have made an opportunity to grow.

Too many investors buy and sell at the worst time. Trying to time the market is the worst thing an investor can do. It is impossible to time the market, and if anyone says he or she can, that person is either lying or has been extremely lucky. The best strategy is to buy and hold for the long term with an investor mindset. However, it is very important to rebalance your portfolio at least once a year. If you, as the investor, have a 60% stock and 40% bond allocation at the beginning of the year, that doesn't mean it should always remain that way. As you contribute capital throughout the year and market events occur, those particular asset classes will perform differently throughout the year. If you invest a fixed-dollar amount into these asset classes and stocks do better than bonds, you may end up with a 70% stock and 30% bond allocation at the end of the year. You may want to rebalance at that point, depending on the asset allocation mix you prefer.

Rebalancing is simply making sure the portfolio allocations you initially set remain intact. Your investments will perform differently throughout the year. As such, it is likely that your initial portfolio breakdown will shift and change. For example, your initial portfolio comprised of 70% Vanguard Total Stock Market Index Fund Admiral Shares (VTSAX) and 30% Vanguard Total International Stock Index Fund Admiral Shares (VTIAX) may eventually shift throughout the year to 75% Vanguard Total Stock Market Index Fund Admiral Shares (VTSAX) and 25% Vanguard Total International Stock Index Fund Admiral Shares (VTIAX) if Vanguard Total Stock Market Index Fund Admiral Shares (VTSAX) outperformed.

There are two ways to rebalance your portfolio. The first way is to sell your current over-weighted investments and roll the amount into the underweighted investment. In this example, you would sell 5% of Vanguard Total Stock Market Index Fund Admiral Shares (VTSAX) and then buy Vanguard Total International Stock Index Fund Admiral Shares (VTIAX) with the 5%.

The second way to rebalance your portfolio is to change future auto investments allocations by decreasing your dominant position and increasing your less dominant position.

Something to keep in mind is that if these investments are in a retirement account such as an IRA, 401(k), 403(b), etc., you can easily and more quickly handle the rebalance as described in the first example. But for the investments that are in non-retirement accounts, such as taxable brokerage accounts, proceeding with the first step of selling and buying would cause a taxable event. So for non-retirement accounts, I would use the second method to avoid that situation and problem.

So make sure you are checking your portfolio allocation at least once a year. Set a fixed date so you don't forget to check it.

Investment Rule of Thumb: When thinking about your investment portfolio, trying to decide what percentage should be allocated in stocks, use the following equation:

Subtract your current age from 120. That answer should be the percentage of stock allocation in your portfolio.

Examples : $120 - 20 = 100\%$ stock portfolio; $120 - 45 = 75\%$ stock portfolio

Lesson 6: Target Date Fund Diversification

Even with all the knowledge you can glean, it can still be difficult to figure out how to diversify "correctly." There is even a chance that some of your investment products have a high correlation or overlap. If you find it challenging to diversify, a potential option for you would be a target date fund. I personally believe that target date funds are sub-optimal (but not the worst option) as you, the investor, lose the ability to control allocations and the fees tend to be on the higher side compared to alternative options, such as exchange-traded funds (ETFs) or index funds.

Many companies offer a target date fund investment product because it does the asset allocation and rebalancing for you. This is the type of fund that an investor is typically auto-enrolled in within a 401(k). These funds manage the stock and bond mix for you, depending on the date you say you are going to retire. For example, you plan to retire in 2055. When you are younger, target date fund investment products will offer a more aggressive stock-heavy portfolio, but the fund will automatically reallocate to become less risky as the year 2055 approaches and your investment time horizon shrinks. While these funds are often used for targeting retirement, you can also use them for shorter-term goals like a child's education. It's not all on autopilot, however. Two funds with the same target date can have vastly different stock-to-bond allocations. It's important to do your homework and make sure that the mix is inline with your risk tolerance and financial goals.

Lesson 7: Single Asset versus Mutual Fund versus Index Fund versus Exchange-Traded Funds

You know what type of asset classes exist and the diversification that an investor must consider. Let's discuss what type of financial products are available to you to buy and sell. For a start, it is your choice whether to purchase one or many of these asset classes. You can decide to have all five asset classes as part of your portfolio or just one. It is your choice as an investor. The type of account and investment goal will play a large role in this determination. Additionally, you can decide to buy a single asset or a group of assets. If you decide to buy a group of a particular asset class, this is what is called a mutual fund, index fund, or exchange-traded funds (ETFs).

A mutual fund is an investment that pools the individual investor's money with other investors' money to purchase shares of a collection of stocks, bonds, or other assets. Similarly, an ETF is a type of investment fund that is traded on stock exchanges much like other securities. Lastly, an index fund is a mutual fund or exchange-traded fund designed to follow certain guidelines, so the fund can track a specified basket of underlying investments. Mutual funds, index funds, and ETFs can be designed to beat the market, be the market, or even track a specific sector such as technology, healthcare, or information technology stocks.

The two main differences between these types of financial products are that mutual funds are usually actively managed to buy or sell assets within the fund in an attempt to beat the market and help investors profit. ETFs and index funds are mostly passively managed because they typically track a specific market index. ETFs can be bought and sold like stocks, but mutual funds **cannot**. If you as the investor want to buy or sell a mutual fund, you will receive the market price of the asset at the end of that trading day. However, if an investor wants to buy or sell an ETF, you will receive the market price of the asset at the time the investor decides to buy or sell.

There are pros and cons to each. If you buy an individual asset of a company, such as a stock, you may have a higher ceiling because that company asset is not dependent on other companies' assets. But it is also more likely for your stock to experience a larger decrease in value since that company asset is not dependent on other companies' assets. That is why mutual funds, index funds, and ETFs have become so popular in today's investing world. They naturally enhance diversification of a person's portfolio and reduce risk. Remember, you, the investor, have the option to buy whatever asset and investment product you feel is best for your situation.

For example, if you purchased one share of stock in Apple in 2002 for $100, that stock would have grown 130 times its original value investment by mid-2019. On the other hand, if you purchased an S&P 500 index fund during this same timespan, your investment would have only grown at about 2.3 times its original value. From that example, it is easy to be attracted to those historical returns. However, for every Apple, there are 100 failed companies. Interestingly, in an article "Do stocks outperform Treasury bills?," Hendrik Bessembinder, Francis Labriola, and Mary B. Labriola researched and evaluated the returns of all U.S. common stock that was traded in the New York and American stock exchanges as on the NASDAQ, beginning in 1926. The findings "help to explain why active strategies, which tend to be poorly diversified, most often underperform." According to Bessembinder, Labriola, and Labriola, they found that

> the largest returns come from very few stocks overall—just 86 stocks—have accounted for $16 trillion in wealth creation, half of the stock market total, over the past 90 years. All of the wealth creation can be attributed to the thousand top-performing stocks, while the remaining 96% of stocks collectively matched one-month T-bills.
>
> *(Bessembinder et al., 2022)*

Further, when you buy the S&P 500, you are essentially making the decision to BE, or at least to be a part of, the market. Individual stocks and actively managed mutual funds may be able to outperform the market at times, but it has been proven that they do not outperform the market over the long term on a net return (after fees and taxes) basis.

Based on history, it rarely happens as the market employs the law of averages. Historically, the stock market has returned approximately 10%. Using the rule of 72, your investment would double every 7.2 years (72/10%). If you have a 43-year investment life, say, from age 22 to age 65, your money will compound and double about 6 times. That is 43 divided by 7.2 years. This means that if you invested $10,000 at age 25 and never touched it again, your investment would be approximately $640,000 at age 65. Imagine if you are consistently contributing throughout that time period as well. Further, your investment life does not really stop at age 65. That is just a gauge to see how much your investments will be at the beginning of the traditional retirement age. You will only withdraw the amount you need for any given year. The majority of your money will remain invested. As you can tell from our compounding example from Lesson 1 in this chapter, you will experience the greatest effects of compound interest in the later years. Figure 6.9 shows the four layers of index investing, in order of occurrence.

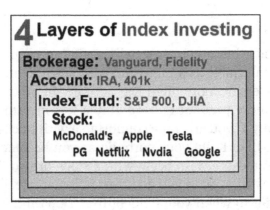

Figure 6.9   Index investing.

Action Plan: Formulating a Plan for Your Investments

Step #1: You need to create a plan early and reap the benefits of compound interest. Don't wait another day, week, month, or year. Every day, week, month, or year that you put off investing is money wasted. It is best to start small—just start. Formulate your plan today.

Step #2: Check your portfolio plan using the stock and asset allocation from the Retirement Rule of Thumb equation discussed in Lesson 5. Subtract your age from 120. That number is the percentage you should allocate for your investment dollars to be put into stock. Since this is a guideline, you also need to keep in mind the type of investor you are. Some people never want to own real estate but want commodities, but others may want the exact opposite or may want more bonds. Maybe you want to just follow Ray Dalio's All Weather Portfolio, which is fine as well.

Step #3: Choose the stocks you want to buy as well as any other investments you are interested in such as bonds, real estate, and/or commodities. Remember that you don't have

(continued)

(continued)

to diversify that much, especially at first or until you become more comfortable as an investor. Also, keep in mind Lesson 5 about diversification: often less is more. In other words, it is usually more prudent to have only a few investments rather than many. If you are more comfortable with stocks, stick with that and then build your portfolio as you become more confident. You can always begin with a stock or two that you are familiar with. Also, if you do invest in real estate, I would suggest doing so when you are debt-free. Don't think about borrowing money to make money. Borrowing money to purchase real estate is counterintuitive.

Step #4: List your portfolio plan here:

_____

_____

_____

_____

_____

_____

_____

_____

_____

_____

_____

_____

Chapter 7

Formulating Your Investment Plan

Now that you have a better understanding of the types of investments at your disposal and even some that you may already have, it is time to really capitalize on the information and put a plan in place to really grow your money. Growing your money will help you reach those long-sought goals and dreams. It will set you and your family up for a secure future. Let's begin to formulate your plan.

Lesson 1: Where to Buy Asset Classes

Knowing the types of assets that are bought and sold along with what type of financial products in which these assets are offered is only part of the picture. You also need to understand where to buy these valuable assets. As the investor, you can buy these asset classes individually or in a bundled financial product through investment accounts or directly from a provider such as Fidelity, Charles Schwab, Vanguard (my personal favorite), or other such providers. Choosing one provider over another is a personal decision. Keep in mind which provider offers more assets, the best investment products to fit your needs and wants, has the lowest fees, the best customer service, and has the best reputation. When you buy an index fund or ETF, you get a diversified selection of securities in one easy, low-cost investment.

Investment Rule of Thumb: To figure out how much to spend in retirement, it is usually safe to say about 4% of your nest egg per year. If your nest egg is $1.5 million, your first year's expenses should be $60k.

Lesson 2: Types of Investment Accounts

Having an understanding of the assets you can buy, the financial-bundled products in which you can buy them, and the providers from which to buy them leads us to another important piece of the puzzle. You must fully understand the types of accounts that you need to have in order to purchase these types of assets. Each account is different from a tax perspective. In general, you can buy these types of financial products in the following types of accounts:

1. 401(k), 403(b), and 457(b)
2. Thrift Savings Plan (TSP)
3. SOLO 401(k)
4. SEP IRA
5. Individual Retirement Account (IRA)
6. Health Savings Account (HSA)
7. Taxable Brokerage Account
8. 529 College Savings Plan
9. Uniform Transfers to Minors Act (UTMA) and Uniform Gifts to Minors Act (UGMA)

401(k), 403(b), and 457(b) Accounts

A 401(k) plan is an employer-sponsored, tax-favored retirement savings account designed for the employees of the company. Employee funding means the money for the account comes directly from an employee's paycheck and some or all of that contribution may be matched by the employer. Definitely check with your employer to see if there is an established 401(k) plan that matches contributions. It is free money and an easy way to invest for your future.

A 403(b) is a U.S. tax-advantaged retirement savings plan available for different organizations such as nonprofit employers, public school teachers, and some nonprofit employers.

A 457(b), like the 401(k), is an employer-sponsored, tax-favored retirement savings account also known as a deferred compensation plan. This plan is offered to firefighters, police officers, and other local government and state employees.

These three accounts have the same purpose, but the major difference between the accounts is to whom the accounts are offered. All the accounts fundamentally operate the same way.

You are probably most familiar with the 401(k) plan, which is a type of investment account. The move from pension plans to the 401(k) plan was corporate America's way of reducing taxes for themselves. In 1978, Congress passed the Revenue Act of 1978 which allowed employees to avoid being taxed on deferred compensation. In short, it allowed companies to save more on taxes. Some pension plans still are in effect today, but many companies are freezing their plans or getting rid of them entirely.

At most companies, employees have the option to set up a 401(k) plan through their full-time employment. Their company offers the 401(k) plan through a brokerage institution like Vanguard, Fidelity, or Charles Schwab, for example. The employee decides how much of each paycheck to contribute and to which investment choices that money will go. Your employer may also choose to make contributions to the plan, but this is optional. If your employer does match, take advantage of that, but don't count this toward your personal contribution. Look on it as an added benefit.

Many companies will auto-enroll new employees in this type of investment account. If you have never accessed your 401(k) but you contribute, I recommend that you get access to this account immediately. New employees are almost always auto-enrolled within a

Target Date Fund at a 6% contribution rate. This may NOT be your best option, as I mentioned in Chapter 6.

Some 401(k) plans will have a Roth and traditional IRA option. You may also hear these 401(k)s being called pre-tax or after-tax. Often you will hear people say they have a "Roth." There is literally no such thing as a *Roth*. For example, let's say you have a blue coat and you tell your friend that you have a "blue." They would likely respond with: "A blue what?" You would follow up and say, "A blue coat." The account is the 401(k) and the type of 401(k) is simply the tax option that the investor has chosen.

The difference between the two comes down to when you pay taxes. With a traditional 401(k), you pay taxes later, but with a Roth 401(k), you pay taxes now. An easy rule of thumb way to choose between the Roth IRA or the traditional IRA is to compare your current tax status with what you think it may be at the age of retirement. If you are in a higher tax bracket now than you will be or think you may be at your retirement age, choosing the traditional IRA probably will make more sense. On the other hand, if you are in a lower tax bracket now than you expect to be at your retirement age, choosing the Roth IRA route might make more sense for you. For those who think predicting your future tax status seems like a complete shot in the dark, you might want to contribute to a traditional IRA account and a Roth IRA account in the same year, assuming your employer offers both options. This would allow you to take advantage of tax benefits both now and later. Personally, I typically prefer a hybrid approach of some sort. I would recommend meeting with a tax professional for tax planning to see what suits your situation best when trying to decide between a Roth IRA or a traditional IRA.

There are limits on the contributions that you are allowed to make and the amounts are subject to change every year. As of 2023, the contribution amount for an IRA (traditional or Roth) is $6,500 with a $1,000 catch-up contribution. For a 401(k), it is $22,500 with a $7,500 catch-up contribution. It is tax-free growth while money is invested.

> **Investment Rule of Thumb: Always take the match. Always! It is FREE money.**

Thrift Savings Plan (TSP)

A TSP is a contribution plan for U.S. civil service employees and retirees along with any member of the uniformed services such as the Army, Navy, or Marines.

A TSP is also a defined contribution plan and resembles a 401(k). Two major differences are who the plan is offered to and the types of investments available within the plan. As with a 401(k) plan that allows the participant to invest in multiple types of investment funds offered by the specific plan, TSP participants are limited to the following six investing options. The investment options are somewhat restricted compared to other types of investment accounts, limiting participants to only six funds like a G Fund, which is a Government Securities Investment. The six funds that are available are:

1. Government Securities Investment Fund (G Fund)
2. Fixed-Income Investment Index Fund (F Fund)
3. Common Stock Index Investment Fund (C Fund)
4. Small-Capitalization Stock Index Fund (S Fund)
5. International Stock Index Investment Fund (I Fund)
6. Lifecycle Funds (L Funds).

Government Securities Investment Fund (G Funds) are for federal employees with TSP accounts and are noted as being low risk, yet it also has the lowest rate of return to date compared to the other funds. While the rate of return is low, it will never be a negative return.

Fixed-Income Investment Index Fund (F Fund) is a good option for active and retired U.S. civil service employees who want diversification in their fund, low risk along with capital preservation, which is a method of handling investments, so the amount invested will be protected from losses and will gain in value. This method attempts to reduce risk over maximizing gains.

Common Stock Index Investment Fund (C Fund) is the best match for those who are interested in a fund that attempts to match the outcomes and performance of the S&P 500 Index, thus providing the participant with equity ownership in midsize and large U.S. company stocks. This provides the possibility of high investment returns over the long term.

Small-Capitalization Stock Index Fund (S Fund) is similar to the C Fund except it does not match the performance of the S&P 500 but rather the Dow Jones Index which is invested in small and medium-sized U.S. companies. The companies in the Dow Jones Index are those excluded from the S&P 500 Index. This fund has a higher change of volatility than the C Fund but there is more potential for higher investment returns.

International Stock Index Investment Fund (I Fund) provides an opportunity to invest in non-U.S. companies rather than those in the Dow Jones Index and the S&P 500 and, as such, is a good opportunity to diversify.

Lifecycle Funds (L Funds) are plans that are a mix of all the plans and are similar to target-date funds. This means that they are invested in growth assets.

The upside to a TSP is that it actually makes investing much easier for the TSP holder. There are also contribution limits within this plan that change from year to year but currently are the same as a 401(k) with a matching component similar to that with a 401(k).

Investment Rule of Thumb: You can figure out the amount of money you need to be financially free by multiplying the amount you spend on an annual basis by 25. The result of that equation is your financial freedom amount:

Example: $50,000 \times 25 = \$1.25$ million

> **So, the amount of money you need to be financially free is $1,250,000.**

SOLO 401(k)

Individuals who are self-employed may qualify for a SOLO 401(k). These include the ownership and/or operation of a profit-generating sole proprietorship, limited liability company (LLC), C corporation, S corporation, or limited partnership that intends to make significant plan contributions. My company, Budgetdog, is an S corporation, so I have a SOLO 401(k). A SOLO 401(k) maximizes retirement savings if you're self-employed or a business owner with no employees other than a spouse. The business owner can contribute as an employer and as an employee.

There are employer contribution limits to the SOLO 401(k). For reference, currently for the 2023 tax year, employers can make contributions up to 25% of compensation, but they cannot exceed $66,000. Generally, the contributions are business expense deductions.

Contributions are not required every year. However, when the contributions are made, it is mandatory that all participants receive the same percentage.

Just as there are employer contribution limits to the SOLO 401(k), there are also limits to employee contributions. For 2023, it is legal for employees to defer all of their compensation up to $22,500. However, for those who are 50 years of age or older, the maximum is $30,000. Of course, those amounts are subject to change each year, but this gives you a point of reference.

It is possible for those with SOLO 401(k) plans to make pre-tax contributions or after-tax contributions and roll-over of pre-tax assets are allowed. It is expected that beginning 2024, any catch-up contributions made will have to be made as after-tax contributions known as Roth plans. The exception to this will be for those with $145,000 or less in compensation as adjusted for inflation.

SEP IRA

A SEP IRA is similar to a SOLO 401(k) with a few exceptions. This plan allows the participant to save 25% of his or her income in the account, unlike the SOLO plans in which participants have the ability to save up 100% as the employee contribution, up to the annual specified limit, and then up to 25% as an employer contribution. Also, a SOLO 401(k) plan enables the participant to save money more quickly, but it is allowable for businesses with only one person employed or with a spouse.

Individual Retirement Account (IRA)

An IRA is an investment account that many people are familiar with as it sets aside money for retirement savings. The biggest difference between an IRA and a 401(k) is that an IRA is not sponsored by an employer, so it is an investor's option whether or not to open an IRA. Investors can enroll in an IRA through brokerage institutions. My personal favorite is Vanguard because Vanguard traditionally has the lowest fees, exceptional customer service, has fantastic investment options, and is one of the best-known brokerage institutions.

IRA plans also have a Roth (pre-tax) or a traditional (after-tax) option. We have previously discussed these. Like many investment plans, there are contribution limits of $6,500 in 2023 and these are subject to change each year. The IRS updates these limits annually.

One fantastic feature about Roth IRAs is that a person can open a Roth IRA for anyone who meets the specified criteria. This is a magnificent way to begin saving for your children's future as well. If your child has earned income for which your child receives a W-2, a parent may open a custodial IRA and actually begin contributing to that IRA. The limitation is that the parent who wants to begin the child's Roth IRA may do so as long as the child has at least as much earned income as the total contribution amount. Imagine beginning an investment account for your child at 14 years of age. The additional years could result in hundreds of thousands of dollars, maybe even millions of dollars in the long run.

Although the contribution limits are much lower than with the 401(k) plan, I consider a Roth IRA superior to a 401(k) because 401(k)s on average have higher fees. Therefore, I usually support having both an IRA and a 401(k) when it comes to investing for retirement.

Health Savings Account (HSA)

An HSA is a medical savings account that has a tax advantage for those who are enrolled in a high-deductible health plan. It provides a triple tax advantage. The first is that the funds go in tax-free. If you then invest that money in a mutual fund within the HSA, that money also grows tax-free. The third layer is that as long as you use the money for eligible medical expenses, that money is not taxed.

HSAs are my personal favorite, and I think it is the best investment account, tax-wise, available. I use an HSA as a third account for retirement, but many investors use an HSA strictly for medical purposes. Remember these are only available to those who have a high-deductible health plan. If you do not have such a plan, an HSA is not available to you.

However, for those who are eligible, an HSA works like the other investment accounts except that there is a required cash reserve. Most accounts require at least $1,000 in cash before you can invest.

The question is how investors can use an HSA for retirement. Here is how I navigate that. I pay for all medical costs out of pocket and save my receipts. Then at retirement age, I will use these receipts to withdraw up to that amount tax-free. You must save every receipt. Additionally, if you do use this for medical expenses, you can still use the leftover amount at retirement. The 2023 HSA contribution limit for a single individual is $3,850. A family can contribute $7,750. However, for those who are 55 years of age and older, there is a catch-up contribution amount of an additional $1,000. These amounts and limits are subject to change annually since they are established by the IRS.

Taxable Brokerage Account

This is the last type of investment account that we need to discuss. A Taxable Brokerage Account is an arrangement in which an investor deposits money with a licensed brokerage firm that places trades on behalf of the investor. Even though the brokerage firm places the orders, the assets from the transactions belong to the investor. The investor usually must claim the capital gains that incur from the executed trade as taxable income.

You can set up a Taxable Brokerage Account in any brokerage institution.

One of the appeals of a Taxable Brokerage Account is that these accounts aren't designed for only one way, so an investor can utilize it in many ways. Therefore, some investors use a Taxable Brokerage Account simply as a savings account for intermediate to long-term goals. Many investors use it as another great investment account. Others use it as a bridge for retirement, which is one of the ways I personally use it. While there are a few early withdrawal strategies from retirement accounts such as Roth conversion ladders, Rule of 55, or 72(t), the Taxable Brokerage Account serves as an easier and more practical way to access investment money prior to age 59.5. Lastly, some may even use it as a child savings vehicle that they gift to their children later (which is subject to the gift tax exclusion amounts established by the IRS and are subject to change annually). This account remains in the parent's name, giving them ultimate control of the funds until it is later gifted. We use this account as an alternative to the UTMA account option (discussed later in this lesson) so that we retain control. You may have multiple brokerage accounts and there is no limit to how much money you can invest in those accounts. I personally like to open one account for each goal. Therefore, we have one for early retirement as well as two separate brokerages for both of my daughters that we invest in.

When it comes to a Taxable Brokerage Account, there are taxes associated with it that differ from tax-efficient accounts such as retirement accounts, a 529 College Savings Account (discussed next), or a Health Savings Account (HSA). The gains investors receive from these accounts consist of capital appreciation, which is the increase in asset price and dividends from corporation or interest income such as a bond. Each type of gain is taxed differently.

Capital Gains Appreciation

This is money earned from capital gains and is taxed at different rates, depending on how long you hold the investment. Gains on investments held for one year or less before selling are short-term capital gains and are taxed as ordinary income. Holding an asset for more than one year allows you to have a more favorable tax treatment on the gains when you sell. Gains that you hold over a year, called long-term capital gains, are taxed at a lower rate than short-term capital gains and can range anywhere from zero to 20%. This is dependent upon your personal income tax bracket. The pay-off is to invest for a longer amount of time and reap the tax reward associated with that compared to investing for short periods of time.

Dividends

Dividends that an investor receives are classified as being qualified or unqualified. Qualified dividends are taxed using lower, long-term capital gains tax rates. Unqualified dividends are taxed as ordinary income at your income tax rate. Most of the time, dividends fall into the category of qualified dividends. If a particular company fails to pay corporate taxes on profits, that company is deemed unqualified. This is something that investors may see more of in an investment such as a REIT.

Interest

Investors earn interest through a bond, CDs, or as cash held in brokerage accounts. When you earn interest on any investment from a bond, certificate of deposit, or just from holding cash in your brokerage account, the income is generally taxed as ordinary income.

One Tip

One tip for when you are beginning your investment journey, it is to your advantage to hold your REITs (unqualified dividend) and bonds (interest) in a retirement account as opposed to a non-retirement account due to the tax treatment. Within a Taxable Brokerage Account, both of these are taxed at your ordinary income tax rate, whereas there are no taxes accrued within a retirement account.

529 College Savings Plan

Another investment plan, the 529 College Savings Plan, is a tax-advantaged investment plan designed to encourage saving for future education expenses for a person who is the designated beneficiary. Typically they are used for college, but these can also be used for kindergarten to high school.

A 529 College Savings Plan, often referred to as a 529, is offered through all 50 states, but some states have better plans than others. In all but seven states, a portion or sometimes even the full amount of a taxpayer's 529 College Savings Plan contribution is deductible when computing state income tax. California, Delaware, Hawaii, Kentucky, Maine, New Jersey, and North Carolina have a state income tax but do not offer a deduction for contribution. 529s are fantastic options since the earnings in a 529 College Savings Plan grow tax-free on the federal level and will not be taxed when the money is taken out to pay for education.

Another benefit of a 529 College Savings Plan is that an investor can open an account for a child who is not even born yet. You simply open the account and list yourself as the beneficiary. When the child is born, you need to update the beneficiary information. This allows investors to take care of the compound growth of being in the market for a longer time period than the typical 18-year time period.

What happens if dependents get a scholarship? In that situation, you are able to withdraw that scholarship portion tax-free. Another nice feature is that you are permitted to change the beneficiary to a grandchild's name at that point if it is necessary. Keep in mind that doing that does incur a 10% penalty.

Contribution limits of a 529 College Savings Plan vary from state to state, but the limits are all high. For example, in my state of Texas, currently the annual limit is $500,000. If you are curious, you can easily do a Google search to find your state's contribution limit. Currently, Vanguard has a website that allows you to click any state to find out specifics about that state's 529 plan. I have added that link under Resources.

Beginning in 2024, the Secure Act 2.0 will impose a $35,000 limit that you can roll from a 529 to a Roth IRA. Prior to Secure Act 2.0, you were unable to roll money from a 529 to a Roth IRA. The roll-over must be to the beneficiary and the Roth IRA must be open for at least 15 years. Rollovers are also subject to standard IRA contribution limits. Lastly, according to the Secure Act 2.0, beginning in 2024, a person can't roll over any contributions or earnings in the last five years of the plan.

Figure 7.1 presents a summary of the key points of the different investment accounts.

> **Investing Rule of Thumb: Make sure you invest in your retirement before you invest in your child's education. A child can get scholarships for school, but there is no such thing as a scholarship for retirement. So, invest in your own future first.**

Uniform Transfers to Minors Act (UTMA) and Uniform Gifts to Minors Act (UGMA)

Uniform Transfers to Minors Act, UTMA for short, is an Act drafted in 1986 that permits minors to own different types of property. This property includes things such as fine art and real estate. Patents and royalties are also permitted under UTMA. It allows for the transfer of the property to take place through inheritance. The Uniform

	Taxable Brokerage Account	Traditional 401(k)	Roth 401(k)	Solo 401(k)	Traditional IRA	Roth IRA	
What's the purpose of the account?	**Anything.** The most flexible account.	**Save for retirement**	**Save for retirement**	**Save for retirement**	**Save for retirement**	**Save for retirement**	
How are contributions taxed?	Contributions are made with post-tax dollars.	Contributions are made with pre-income-tax dollars. a.k.a. "tax deferred." You still have to pay Social Security and Medicare taxes. Employer contributions are not taxed.	Contributions are made with post-tax dollars. Employer contributions are not taxed, but are contributed to your traditional 401(k) account, not to your Roth 401(k) account.	Can follow either Roth or Traditional taxation.	Contributions are made with pre-income-tax dollars. a.k.a. "tax deferred" You still have to pay Social Security and Medicare taxes.	Contributions are made with post-tax dollars.	
How are withdrawals taxed?	Withdrawals are taxed according to capital gains tax brackets.	Withdrawals are taxed according to federal and state income tax brackets.	Withdrawals are not taxed.	Can follow either Roth or Traditional taxation.	Withdrawals are taxed according to federal and state income tax brackets.	Withdrawals are not taxed.	
How is investment growth taxed?	Realized growth (a.k.a. once investments are sold) within the account is subject to capital gains tax.	Growth within the account is not taxed.	Growth within the account is not taxed.	Growth within the account is not taxed.	Growth within the account is not taxed.	Growth within the account is not taxed.	
How are dividends taxed?	Dividends are taxed annually. Some dividends are subject to income tax. Others are subject to capital gains tax.	Dividends within the account are not taxed.	Dividends within the account are not taxed.	Dividends within the account are not taxed.	Dividends within the account are not taxed.	Dividends within the account are not taxed.	
Any age-based limits? Withdrawals? RMDs? Etc.	There are no age-based limits.	You cannot withdraw funds until age 59.5, without penalty. Required Minimum Distributions begin at age 72. Some caveats and exceptions apply.	You cannot withdraw funds until age 59.5, without penalty. Required Minimum Distributions begin at age 72. Some caveats and exceptions apply.	You cannot withdraw funds until age 59.5, without penalty. Required Minimum Distributions begin at age 72. Some caveats and exceptions apply.	You cannot withdraw funds until age 59.5, without penalty. Required Minimum Distributions begin at age 72. Some caveats and exceptions apply.	You can withdraw contributions at any time. You cannot withdraw gains until age 59.5, without penalty. No RMDs. Some caveats and exceptions apply.	

Figure 7.1   A summarized graph of the key points of different investment accounts.

	403(b) and 457 Accounts	SEP IRA & SIMPLE IRA	529 Plan	Health Savings Account	Flexible Spending Account	UTMA/UGMA
	Save for retirement 403(b) - for public school teachers and certain 501(3)c tax-exempt orgs 457 - state and local gov'ts, and some non-profits.	**Save for retirement**	**Save for K-12/college expenses**	**Save for healthcare expenses** **(can be "converted" to retirement savings eventually)**	**Save for healthcare expenses**	**Gift to children (e.g. for college)** Custodial accounts that transfer assets to a minor without establishing a trust
	Typically, same as Traditional 401(k) Though, some are same as Roth 401(k).	Contributions are made with pre-income-tax dollars. a.k.a. "tax deferred" You still have to pay Social Security and Medicare taxes.	Contributions are made with post-tax dollars.	Contributions are made with pre-income-tax dollars. a.k.a. "tax deferred" You still have to pay Social Security and Medicare taxes.	Contributions are made with pre-income-tax dollars. a.k.a. "tax deferred" You still have to pay Social Security and Medicare taxes.	Contributions are made with post-tax dollars.
	Typically, same as Traditional 401(k) Though, some are same as Roth 401(k).	Withdrawals are taxed according to federal and state income tax brackets.	Withdrawals are not taxed as long as they are used for qualified education expenses.	Withdrawals are not taxed as long as they are used for qualified health expenses.	Withdrawals are not taxed as long as they are used for qualified health expenses.	Withdrawals are not taxed.
	Growth within the account is not taxed.	Growth within the account is not taxed.	Growth within the account is not taxed.	Growth within the account is not taxed.	Not applicable. FSA funds cannot be invested.	Realized growth (a.k.a. once investments are sold) within the account is subject to tax treatment described directly below.
	Dividends within the account are not taxed.	Dividends within the account are not taxed.	Dividends within the account are not taxed.	Dividends within the account are not taxed.	Not applicable. FSA funds cannot be invested.	For 2023 . . . The first $1250 is not taxed The next $1250 is taxed at the child's tax rate. Everything after is taxed at the adult's tax rate.
	403b - You cannot withdraw funds until age 59.5, without penalty. **457** - You can withdraw funds before age 59.5 without penalty, under certain circumstances. Required Minimum Distributions begin at age 72. Some caveats and exceptions apply.	You cannot withdraw funds until age 59.5, without penalty. Required Minimum Distributions begin at age 72. Some caveats and exceptions apply.	You can withdraw contributions at any time to pay for qualified educational expenses.	You can withdraw contributions at any time to pay for qualified health expenses. Note: you can even hold onto receipts for **years** and then "refund yourself" later. This can be useful to let your HSA funds grow as much as possible.	You can withdraw contributions at any time to pay for qualified expenses. **Important:** FSAs have a "use it, or lose it" feature. Unlike all other accounts here, you must use FSA funds in the year.	UTMA/UGMAs are **irrevocable**. Once money is in the account, it can only be withdrawn in two ways: 1) The account custodian withdraws it directly on behalf of the beneficiary child 2) The beneficiary has reached the age of majority (varies by state) and withdraws it themselves.

	Taxable Brokerage Account	Traditional 401(k)	Roth 401(k)	Solo 401(k)	Traditional IRA	Roth IRA	
What investments are available?	Just about anything on the market.	Typically only those offered by the 401k plan administration	Typically only those offered by the 401k plan administration.	Typically, you (as the business owner) can work with a 401(k) administrator to access a wide range of potential investments ... but you likely cannot change investment options on short notice.	Just about anything on the market.	Just about anything on the market.	
Are there contribution limits?	There are no contributions limits.	For 2023 ... $22,500 per year if under age 50 $30,000 per year if over age 50	For 2023 ... $22,500 per year if under age 50 $30,000 per year if over age 50.	For 2023 ... $66,000 per year if under age 50 $73,500 per year if over age 50.	For 2023 ... $6500 per year if under age 50 $7500 per year if over age 50.	For 2023 ... $6500 per year if under age 50 $7500 per year if over age 50.	
Are there eligibility limits?	There are no eligibility limits for adults. Children, typically, cannot set up their own brokerage accounts.	Yes—the account must be created and funded through your employer.	Yes—the account must be created and funded through your employer.	Must be a business owner with only one employee (yourself)—although you can include your spouse as an extra employee.	Yes. If you are a 401(k) participant through work, your IRA benefits phase out between: Single: $68K–$78K Married Filing Jointly: $109K–$129K Non-active participant married to active: $204K–$214K.	Roth phaseouts are: Single: $129K–$144K Married filing jointly: $204K–$214K.	
Are there withdrawal penalties?	There are no withdrawal penalities.	Yes, if withdrawals are made before age 59.5, a 10% penalty tax is assessed, in addition to the income taxes mentioned above. Certain caveats and exceptions apply.	Yes, if withdrawals are made before age 59.5, a 10% penalty tax is assessed, in addition to the income taxes mentioned above. Certain caveats and exceptions apply.	Yes, if withdrawals are made before age 59.5, a 10% penalty tax is assessed, in addition to the income taxes mentioned above. Certain caveats and exceptions apply.	Yes, if withdrawals are made before age 59.5, a 10% penalty tax is assessed, in addition to the income taxes mentioned above. Certain caveats and exceptions apply.	Yes, if gains are withdrawn before age 59.5, a 10% penalty tax is assessed. Certain caveats and exceptions apply.	

Figure 7.1 Continued

	403(b) and 457 Accounts	SEP IRA & SIMPLE IRA	529 Plan	Health Savings Account	Flexible Spending Account	UTMA/UGMA
	Typically only those offered by the plan administration.	Just about anything on the market.	Typically only those offered by the plan administration.	Typically only those offered by the plan administration.	Not applicable. FSA funds cannot be invested.	UGMA—stocks, bonds, funds, etc. UTMA - the same, plus real estate, jewelry, art, etc.
	For 2023 . . . $22,500 per year if under age 50 $30,000 per year if over age 50.	For 2023 . . . SEP - $66,000, **but only from employer** SIMPLE - $15.5K + (if over 50) $3.5K more, + up to 3% employer match.	None, **although** 529 contributions are considered completed gifts (Federal Tax purposes). $17K/year per donor is the 2023 gift exclusion ($34K/year for married couple).	For 2023 . . . $3850 for single $7750 for families and $1000 for "catch up" if 55 or older.	For 2023 . . . $3050 for single $6100 if both spouses have FSAs $5000 for one FSA, if for a family.	None, although UTMA/UGMA contributions are considered completed gifts (Federal Tax purposes). $17K/year per donor is the 2023 gift exclusion ($34K/year for married couple).
	Yes—the account must be created and funded through your employer.	Accounts can only be created by **employers**. That said, self-employed can create these accounts for themselves. Typically seen as a "easy substitute" for more complex 401(k) plans.	No. Anyone with future educational expenses can open a 529 account.	Yes. Only participants enrolled in a high-deductible health plan (HDHP) can contribute to an HSA.	Yes. Only employers can open an FSA on your behalf.	Must be opened by an adult (the custodian) on behalf of a minor (the beneficiary).
	Yes, if withdrawals are made before age 59.5, a 10% penalty tax is assessed, in addition to the income taxes mentioned above. Certain caveats and exceptions apply.	Yes, if withdrawals are made before age 59.5, a 10% penalty tax is assessed, in addition to the income taxes mentioned above. Certain caveats and exceptions apply.	If withdrawals are not used for qualified educational expenses, they are subject to a 10% penalty on top of income taxes.	If withdrawals are not used for qualified health expenses. they are subject to income tax. Additionally, if this occurs prior to age 65, an additional 20% penalty tax is assessed.	At the beginning of the year, you have immediate access to withdrawing your FSA account, *even if you haven't fully funded your account yet!*	None, except that all withdrawals from a custodial account must be for the direct benefit of the beneficiary.

	Taxable Brokerage Account	Traditional 401(k)	Roth 401(k)	Solo 401(k)	Traditional IRA	Roth IRA	
Who owns the account?	Brokerage accounts can be opened for individuals or jointly across many equal owners.	Your contributions to a 401(k) are yours, and yours alone. The "company match" may be subject to vesting/ clawback rules, where the employer has rights to that money for a period of time.	Your contributions to a 401(k) are yours, and yours alone. The "company match" may be subject to vesting/ clawback rules, where the employer has rights to that money for a period of time.	Your contributions to a 401(k) are yours, and yours alone.	You do, 100%.	You do, 100%.	
Other thoughts?	Since there are no limits, this could very well end up being your largest account by the time you retire.	GET YOUR EMPLOYER MATCH! IT'S FREE MONEY! VERY rarely does a scenario arise where the employer match is not worth pursuing.	GET YOUR EMPLOYER MATCH! IT'S FREE MONEY! VERY rarely does a scenario arise where the employer match is not worth pursuing.				

Figure 7.1 Continued

	403(b) and 457 Accounts	SEP IRA & SIMPLE IRA	529 Plan	Health Savings Account	Flexible Spending Account	UTMA/UGMA
	Your contributions to a 403(b)/457 are yours, and yours alone. The "company match" may be subject to vesting/clawback rules, where the employer has rights to that money for a period of time.	You do, 100%.	You own the account and control the investments. A named beneficiary (i.e. the student) will receive the funds for their education.	You do, 100%.	Your employer owns the account, even though you've agreed to fund it from your paychecks.	The custodian owns the account until the beneficiary reaches the age of majority.
	Beware: many 403(b) and 457 plans allow outside "advising" from (predatory) financial professionals.		Reported on FAFSA as a parent's asset, reducing financial aid by up to 5.64% of the account balance. Beneficiaries can be swapped between children and grandchildren.	HSA accounts can provide **triple** tax benefits . . . No tax on contributions. No tax on gains. No tax on qualified withdrawals.	If you leave your employer, you will forfeit your FSA account balance.	Reported on FAFSA as a child's asset, reducing financial aid by up to 20% of the account balance.

Action Plan: Planning Your Investments

1. **Step #1:** Define which investment accounts you need based on your situation. If you are unsure, speak with an investment professional.
2. **Step #2:** Using the following information, see what applies and how you can add any of these to your portfolio. Here is a general framework of investment accounts according to my professional opinion that you may consider and the order:
   a. A 401(k), 403(b), or a 457(b). Invest up to the match amount.
   b. The next investment should be to max out a Roth IRA or a traditional IRA.
   c. If you have more income available, add more to the 401(k), 403(b), or a 457(b) to reach 15% of your gross income.
   d. If it applies to your situation, layer with an HSA and max it out.
   e. Next, add a Taxable Brokerage Account that aligns with your investment goals. It has an unlimited contribution amount.
   f. Lastly, after you fully set yourself up, consider any child investing, such as 529 (if applicable).

Gifts to Minors Act (UGMA) goes back even farther in its inception to 1956, then was revised in 1966, and allows assets such as securities that have been provided to the minor, so all possessions and control of the property is to be held in a custodian's name. This is to the benefit of the minor because an attorney is not needed to set up this type of trust fund.

UTMA and UGMA, like the 529 College Savings Plan, are two other ways to help your child or children. These are investment plans designed to provide additional assets to an investor's child(ren) or grandchildren. However, this can be somewhat complicated because any money in custodial accounts of which you are the custodian is considered part of your taxable estate if you are the legal guardian of the child and the child has not yet reached the age of trust termination. (This age varies from state to state but typically ranges from 18 to 21.) Therefore, these accounts are subject to taxation under the custodian's estate.

Another important component of these plans is that the income from a custodial account must be reported on the child's tax return and is taxed at the child's income tax rate under the Kiddie Tax rules, which change yearly. The custodian or guardian is responsible for filing an income tax return on behalf of the child.

To open an UTMA or an UGMA, the donor appoints a custodian who is the trustee and provides the name and Social Security number of the minor, at which time the donor irrevocably "gifts" the money to the trust. This means the donor has made an irreversible decision. This is exactly where the problem lies for some donors because the assets legally become the minor's assets once the minor comes of age and this cannot be changed. This can raise concerns to investors because some question whether or not the minor will be responsible enough at that age to handle this type of gift.

This is why you should consider what the purpose of this savings act really is for. If it is simply education, the 529 College Savings Plan may be a better route for you. If you want to provide your children with a down payment for a home, the UTMA or UGMA may be a better consideration. However, there is also another alternative for an UTMA, which we will discuss in Lesson 7.

Overall, these types of investment accounts provide another opportunity for parents or legal guardians to fast-track their child's or their children's future. The gift tax exclusion amounts are established by the IRS and are subject to change annually.

Lesson 3: Fees: What They Are and Why They Matter So Much

Anyone who has bought an airline ticket, booked an Airbnb or hotel room, or bought a concert ticket is well aware of fees. They all too quickly add up. You think you can fly from one place to another for $74 since that is what your search shows, until you find out that there are all kinds of booking fees, baggage fees even for a carry-on for some carriers, seat fee, etc. That is all before adding in taxes. They drive the cost of the $74 ticket you thought you were getting to your destination to an incredible price, making that quick trip to the beach or the mountains now quite costly.

With investing, it is very much the same. Many investors boast about their investments without factoring in the fees associated with them, just like that $74 ticket to your favorite destination that was much higher than the listed price.

When you hear investors talk about their portfolio return of 10%, 11%, or 12%, that is oftentimes before fees. So, like the airline ticket that is much more costly than you were led to believe or the actual price of a hotel after fees, with investing, fees DO matter.

Fees can single-handedly derail an investor's performance, so you must understand what the different fees are and how to find the fees that you are paying for with your investment gains.

An investor will experience fees at the broker level, account level, and at the asset level and needs to be aware of all fees. To begin, the account that you are invested in that is held at a specific broker is not the investment. The underlying investment is the asset that you select to invest in within that account. Each asset will issue a fund prospectus. A fund prospectus will detail out everything about the asset, particularly the investment objective, price and performance, portfolio management, fees and minimums, and distributions. A fund fact sheet will also provide this information and is usually in easy-to-understand language. This is important because it will list all of the fees that investors are unaware they are paying. Let's use Vanguard 500 Index Fund Admiral Shares, one of the S&P 500 Index funds (VFIAX), as an example. If I wanted to figure out the fees associated with VFIAX, I would use the following steps:

1. I would do a Google search for VFIAX Prospectus. When you do that, VFIAX-Vanguard 500 Index Fund Admiral Shares should come up.

2. Click and open the VFIAX Prospectus on the first link. There
   you will see all of the different fees associated with VFIAX such
   as fund-specific fees, expense-ratio percentage (0.04%), purchase
   fee, fund family redemption fee, and annual account service fee
   (not to worry—I explain what these and other fees are just below).

It is that easy. The fees are all disclosed there for you. Take note
that our example VFIAX, a low-cost index fund, has minimal fees.
As you can see, this investment option has a .04% expense ratio fee
and a $25 annual account service fee for account balances below
$10,000. VFIAX has a fantastic fee structure.

The fund prospectus will detail every single fee and expense
associated with the investment that you own. Since each type of
investment account, even within the same brokerage, and its underlying investments will have different fees, it is imperative to make
sure you understand the account that you are in and the investments that you hold.

The following is the breakdown of common fee types in
many accounts.

- **Expense ratio** is an annual fee that all funds or exchange-
  traded funds (ETFs) charge their shareholders. It expresses the
  percentage of assets deducted each fiscal year for fund expenses,
  including 12b-1 fees, management fees, plan administration
  fees, operating costs, and all other asset-based costs incurred
  by the fund. Expense ratio usually is the largest expense eating away at your real returns because it incorporates several of
  the expenses listed below. The average expense ratio for actively
  managed mutual funds is between 0.5% and 1.0%. Some may
  be lower (recall, VFIAX expense ratio is .04%) and they rarely
  exceed 2.5%. For passive index funds, the typical ratio is about
  0.2%. Let's take a closer look at several of the fees that fall under
  the expense ratio:
  - The first is the 12b-1 fee. It kind of seems like we are back to
    all of the hidden airline and hotel fees here. With 12b-1 fees,
    think of this as the annual marketing or distribution fee on

a mutual fund. They are the fees that are paid out of the mutual fund for a variety of costs such as distribution, marketing, selling, and costs incurred to provide the shareholder services. The 12b-1 fee is an operational expense. Typically the 12b-1 fees range from 0.25% to 0.75%, which is the maximum allowed of a fund's net assets. This is just a piece of the expense ratio.

- Management fees are a fee charged as a percentage of the total assets managed. These can often be at least partially paid with pre-tax or tax-deductible dollars. For example, an investment advisor who charges a 1% management fee means that for every $100,000 invested, you will pay $1,000 per year in advisory fees.
- Plan administration are fees that you pay because whether it's a bank or another financial institution, someone is managing your 401(k). Plan administration fees cover general management like record-keeping, accounting, legal, and trustee services. It also contributes to any additional services that you may have access to like customer service representatives, educational seminars, and electronic access to plan information. Some employers pay this fee for account holders, but it's usually passed on to you in the form of a flat fee or a percentage of the total balance.
- **Transaction fee** is a fee for each time an order to buy or sell a mutual fund or stock is placed. Transaction fees can range from $9.95 to over $50 per trade. If you are investing small amounts of money, transaction fees can add up quickly. The turnover ratio of an investment usually gives you good insight into what is likely taken out per year. This amount is deducted from the fund's assets. For example, a $50 transaction fee on a $5,000 investment is 1%.
- **Front-end load fee** is a sales charge or commission that an investor pays "upfront," or upon purchase of the asset. The percentage paid for the front-end load varies among investment companies but typically falls within a range of 3.75–5.75%.
- **Back-end load fee** is a fee paid by investors when selling mutual fund shares and is expressed as a percentage of the value of the

fund's shares. A back-end load fee can be a flat fee or gradually decrease over time, usually within 5–10 years.

- **Individual service fees** are additional administrative fees that cover features you opt into like taking out a 401(k) loan, rolling 401(k) investments over to an IRA, or seeking financial advisory services. They are charged separately to participant accounts whenever the participant takes advantage of a certain feature. Before you do anything beyond the basic buying and selling within your 401(k), you need to check whether the individual service will incur a fee and, if it does, how much it will cost for that service.

- **Brokerage fee** is the fee the broker holding your investment account charges. These fees include annual fees to maintain the account, fees to access various trading platforms, the cost for subscriptions to access premium research or investing information, or even fees for inactivity due to infrequent trading in the account. Often if you have the right broker, you can avoid brokerage fees. You will choose your broker based on who is the most well respected, provides the largest variety of assets, the best investment products, the lowest fees, and the best customer services. This is going to be a personal choice. Take your time to find the right broker for you.

- **Management or advisory fee** typically is a percentage of assets under management that the investor pays to a financial advisor or robo-advisor. If you decide to use a financial advisor, it is important you ask the advisor you are working with how his or her compensation package is structured. You are not asking how much they make, so it is not a rude or personal question. The financial advisor should answer the question honestly if he or she is the true "fiduciary" that the advisor claims to be.

- **Redemption fee** is a fee that some funds will charge a shareholder when investors sell or redeem their mutual fund shares; the fee is paid to a broker. This fee is not the same as back-end load and is in addition to them. They must be paid to the fund, generally limited to 2% of the sales amount by the U.S. Securities and Exchange Commission (see Redemption Fee, n.d., in the References).

- **Exchange fee** is the cost or the fee that shareholders are charged if they exchange or transfer to a different fund that is within the same fund grouping.
- **Purchase fee** is incurred by the shareholder and is the fee that some funds charge when investors buy mutual fund shares. This is not the same as a front-end load. Purchase fees may be in addition to front-end load fees.

Let's take a look at some numbers to put all of this into perspective. For this example, we are going to imagine what would happen if you invested $1,250 into your investment accounts each month for 20 years. Over that span, you would have contributed $300,000. We are also going to assume that your investment of $300,000 had an average annual return of 7%. Depending on the amount of fees you were paying, here is the breakdown of each set of fees:

1.0% of fees: cost $198,768
1.5% of fees: cost $285,579
2.0% of fees: cost $364,918
3.0% of fees: cost $503,571

Can you even believe how much of an impact a small 2% fee made in this example? Think about the amount lost in fees if you were to invest much more over time. Is it starting to make sense?

Where I see investors make the two biggest mistakes is in **advisor fees** and **negligence**. Regarding advisor fees, investors will often look to a nicely dressed professional in a swanky office for guidance. There is nothing wrong with that, and I am not saying to avoid this route if you feel that it would help your market performance. However, my advice when seeking a professional for investments is that 90% of investors can educate themselves on the markets just like you are doing right now and can build their own portfolio of investments.

The problem typically lies in the investor's behavior and risk profile. So when deciding whether or not to use a financial professional for investment advice, you, the investor, should fully understand your behavior tendencies and risk profile. If someone is not comfortable with a market drawdown and witnesses a portfolio drop of 20%, does that investor react and sell the investments or does the investor stand strong and let the storm pass? If you would react, and, therefore, sell out of your position, it may be wise to hire a financial professional like the one in the nice three-piece suit in the posh office. Just realize that if you do that, you will be paying an advisor fee for your investment.

A study conducted by Vanguard "suggests that the investor using an advisor gains 1.5% per year over and above the advisor's fee, which would be 2.5% above the average investor who is not using an advisor" (Van Knapp, 2017).

I believe those numbers are fairly accurate, however, I also think the results are skewed because there are many investors without a professional advisor who make horrendous decisions and fail miserably, bringing down the averages for the investor without a professional. Most investors without a professional advisor are simply uneducated, and, therefore, perform much worse than the investor with a professional. I often look at an advisor as an investment therapist. You will need to assess for yourself based on your own behavior and risk tolerance as well as your relationship with money whether or not a professional advisor is right for you.

For **negligence**, it is all too common that investors do not educate themselves on the fees in their portfolios. When an investor does not take the time to educate himself or herself, the investor loses in the end and sometimes in a devastating way. This usually happens because the investors do not review their investments enough. Ironically, these same investors are usually quick to notice a bank fee, so why aren't these investors noticing a 401(k) fee? It is usually because the individual investor does not spend enough time looking at the portfolios of Investments and understanding what is involved. Once the investor is able to make this monumental shift, the investment returns will increase substantially. Understand what you are paying and adjust accordingly. However, simply taking the time to spend 6 months with me in Budgetdog Academy will provide you the education and confidence to run your own investments and avoid these expensive fees. Education pays dividends and, as you can see, fees matter! Just like all of those hidden costs with concert tickets, hotels, and airfares, fees are a secret, insidious investment killer, so be aware.

Lesson 4: When to Invest

One of the most common questions about investing is when to begin investing. The answer essentially is **NOW**, or once all your bad debt, outside of your mortgage, is paid off first, and you have a fully funded emergency fund of 3–6 months of monthly expenses. I recommend this because it is essential to follow these steps to ensure your personal finance situation for long-term performance. Once you have fully addressed bad debt payoff and a fully funded emergency fund, it is time to begin investing.

The three most important factors in an individual's market performance, which I call the wealth triangle (Figure 7.2), are time, amount invested, and the asset to return percentage or net return. With time, remember it is the beauty of compound interest that helps grow your money. Of course, it is easy to understand how significant the amount invested is in the equation. The net return, however, is subject to the market fluctuations. One investment strategy that is proven to work in all economic climates is dollar cost averaging. Dollar cost averaging is when the investor purchases the

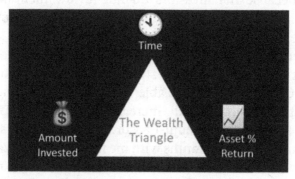

Figure 7.2   Investment factors for the wealth triangle.

same dollar amount of a specific investment over a specified period of time (bi-weekly, monthly, etc.). The aim of dollar cost averaging is to reduce your risk of market volatility and, in fact, to capitalize on market volatility. You can easily calculate your asset return rate by using an investment calculator such as the one at Calculator.net.

Lesson 5: How Much to Invest

To help determine the amount to invest when planning for retirement, I, along with many other professionals, recommend investing a minimum of 15% of your annual gross income. While you can certainly invest more, I firmly believe 15% will allow you to retire comfortably. This is only a general rule, and it may not fit into your specific situation. Therefore, you will want to adjust this to fit your specific needs and goals. This especially applies to those who are already behind in investing and do not have time on their side. For any amount over that 15%, I recommend investing into any of the other investment accounts that best fit your individual situation and preference. For example, you could invest in a Taxable Brokerage Account to use as a bridge investment until retirement, or you could also begin to build a future investment account for your child. There are many options available.

I always recommend investing in low-cost index funds and ETFs. It is really difficult to go wrong with these as you are diversifying, tracking particular pre-identified markets or sectors, and ensuring low costs.

Here is an example using three factors. John is currently 25 years old. His annual gross income is $50,000. He invests $7,500 per year (15% of his annual gross income) into an S&P 500 index fund. The fund gives him a 10% average annual return, and he keeps his money invested like that for 40 years until his retirement. At age 65, John will have an investment account balance of $3.9 million.

In this situation, John definitely benefited from that investment amount. I think it is critical to do that. Personally, I would break down the 15% to retirement as a 401(k) with a company match, a

---

Action Plan: Invest

Step 1: Invest in your 401(k) up to the company match.

Step 2: Max out your IRA annually to the amount as specified by the IRS.

Step 3: Invest the remaining portion in your 401(k) or similar type plan (for the remaining 15%).

---

maxed IRA, and the remaining portion going into another 401(k) or similar plan.

Lesson 6: Risk Profile for Investing

When it comes to investing, one of the most important things to understand is YOURSELF. Just as we discussed the psychology of money, it is also important to know yourself in order to be successful with your investing. In particular, here we are focusing mostly on your risk tolerance. You must be tapped into yourself and the level of risk you are willing to take in order to successfully weather the markets. Your investments will fluctuate. That is what they do. They go up and down naturally but how you react during good times or prosperous times and bad times such as recessions is the single most important factor of investing. And, remember, the more active you are, the less successful you usually are. When we get emotional, we act irrationally, whether it is out of fear or excitement. Whether the market is trending up or trending down, it is important to stay calm. It is easier said than done! Beware!

It is an undeniable fact that we, as humans, will experience emotion during our lifetime, especially when it comes to our money. There is no issue with having emotion, and it can be a great thing most of the time. But we must remember, money does not acknowledge emotion. The earlier we understand this, the better. We need to fully understand our risk tolerance so we can design our investment portfolios around it.

Risk tolerance is defined within our risk profile. This identifies the acceptable level of risk an individual is prepared and able to accept. The willingness to take on risk refers to an individual's risk aversion. Are you risk-neutral, risk-averse, or risk-seeking? Do you have the stomach to handle low, medium, or high risk? If your portfolio experienced a drawdown of 40%, what would you do? In order to figure out what type of risk profile you are, I want you to take a risk profile quiz. There are three that I recommend—Charles Schwab, Vanguard, and JP Morgan—but there are others that are available online that you might also want to try. Links to the three I recommend are in the following Action Plan as well as in the Resources at the end of the book.

Risk tolerance or risk profile is one part of the risk equation. How about your investment horizon? This is another critical piece of investing that you need to keep in mind for successful investing. What is your timeframe? Do you have 10 years until you need to pull your investments or do you have 40 years until you retire? Your age really matters and every account has its own unique timeline. As we know, investments tend to fluctuate. Depending on the portfolio model that you employ, it may fluctuate a lot or a little. This is a key determination in figuring out the risk that you, the investor, is willing to take. Typically, the closer you are to your financial goal, the safer or less risky you want your portfolio to be.

Action Plan

Step #1: Write down whether you think you are risk-averse, risk-neutral, or risk-seeking. Think about different scenarios as well as the individual investments you may want to make. For example, if you have a 529 plan and your child has 15 years before needing the money, does that change your risk profile compared to you personally needing money from your investment in the near future?

(continued)

(continued)

Step #2: Take at least one risk profile questionnaire to figure out what type of risk profile you are, and how the results of it compares to what you think your risk profile is. Keep in mind that if you are sitting in your office, drinking your morning coffee, and are calm, you have a more stable mindset than if you just turned on the news and heard there was a huge stock market crash. So, really try to be honest with yourself and evaluate how you would react about your money. Take one or more of the risk profile quizzes. The three I recommend are:

Charles Schwab Risk Profile Quiz:

`https://www.schwab.com/resource/investment-questionnaire.`

Vanguard Risk Profile Quiz:

`https://investor.vanguard.com/tools-calculators/investor-`
`questionnaire#modal-start-quiz`

JP Morgan Risk Profile Quiz:

`https://am.jpmorgan.com/us/en/asset-management/adv/`
`investment-strategies/model-portfolios/explore-model-`
`portfolios.`

Step #3: Is the result what you expected? Do you agree or disagree? Keep this profile in mind when you are thinking about investing and the types of investment accounts you are thinking of.

Step #4: What is your investment horizon? Calculate the number of years and determine how safe or risky you can be with your investments.

Lesson 7: Investing Framework

Outside of retirement, I would invest as much as possible in other accounts. Everyone has a different situation or goal, so there is no one correct way. There are plenty of options available to the investor, and it is important that you begin as soon as possible. It all begins with your goals. For example, if your number one goal is to retire at 55 years of age, you need to understand the types of accounts that will get you there. If you have a 401(k) at $5 million and no brokerage account, that may not align with your goals.

Here is the six-step process I recommend you do in order to be able to reach your financial goals:

Step 1: List your financial goals, which could be to retire early, to make sure there is money for your children for college, or to be financially independent by a certain age.

Step 2: Ask yourself which accounts you need to use in order to fund your financial goal.

Step 3: Determine at what date you need to achieve your financial goal.

Step 4: Calculate how much money you need in this account by the specified date.

Step 5: Calculate how much money you need to begin investing to reach that financial goal by the specified date.

Step 6: Begin your investment contributions.

Let me walk you through an example scenario, so you can see how this plays out. This is Liam and Quinn's situation and how they planned out their goals. Liam and Quinn have a goal to retire at age 50. They both are 28 years old, and the account that will allow them to retire at that age is a Taxable Brokerage Account. These are Steps 1 and 2.

For Step 3, they determined the date for their early retirement, which will be August 1, 2042. That seems like a long time away, but it really isn't. Step 4, in order to retire 9.5 years earlier than the retirement date designated by the IRS (age 59.5) and to be able to access their retirement accounts, Liam and Quinn determined that they would be able to achieve their financial goal with $2,500,000. They arrived at that amount because they understand the idea of a 4% annual withdrawal in their first year of retirement. (In subsequent years, you adjust the dollar amount you withdraw to account for inflation.) That means they can enjoy a lifestyle of $100,000 per year at that stage in their lives. If they had $2,500,000, they could pull 4% or $100,000 annually. For Step 5, Liam and Quinn calculated that they need to reach $2,500,000 by the time they are 50 years of age (that is 22 years away). They also know that if they invested in a simple S&P 500 fund within a brokerage account earning 10% per year, they would need to invest approximately $2,600 a month to reach their goal.

Their last step, Step 6, was to set up the monthly automatic deduction to invest $2,600 monthly into VFIAX (80% or $2,080) and VTIAX (20% or $520) via Vanguard.

This six-step process is fundamental for all financial goals you have. You will be able to plan confidently for the future. Of course, there are times where life hits you hard, and you may fall off course. This is the power of planning and automation. If you have a good plan in place, you can just re-evaluate your new situation and adjust accordingly. It is much easier to adjust when you have a baseline of where to begin. This plan is calculated so there is no anxiety or fear.

An investment strategy portfolio takeaway is that there is not one size fits all when it comes to investing, as you have learned. However, if I had to recommend one default option as the ideal way to set up an individual's portfolio, the following are the accounts I would include.

First in the portfolio would be some type of employer-sponsored investment. This could include any of the following: 401(k), 403(b), 457(b), an IRA—either Roth or traditional IRA—and a Taxable Brokerage Account.

I would also add on any of the following options: HSA, SOLO 401(k), SEP IRA, and child accounts such as the 529, UTMA, UTGA, Taxable Brokerage, or Roth IRA.

To take this one step further, here is the priority of investment accounts according to my professional opinion:

1. Invest in your workplace plan up to the match (the majority of people will have one of the following: 401(k), 403(b), 457(b), TSP).
2. Max out a Roth IRA or traditional IRA to the annual limit.
3. Invest the remaining up to 15% of your gross income in your workplace plan defined in step 1 above.

4. Max out an HSA to the annual limit.

5. Invest the remaining to a Taxable Brokerage Account.

Within these accounts, here are some rules to always follow. Choose one to five Index funds or ETFs and diversify. Turn on dividend reinvestment. Set up automatic investments—remember to simplify and automate everything. Finally, don't sell anything until you retire.

Action Plan: Organize Your HSA Receipts

Step #1: Upload every medical-related receipt to create a complete record.

Step #2: Save all of your uploaded medical-related receipts in an email folder. This is especially helpful when saving receipts over time such as for an HSA because paper receipts are likely to get lost or crumpled up. You need to keep exact accounting, so you are best to make sure you do not try to have physical copies.

Step #3: Label these clearly and accurately to make it easy for you when completing tax forms. Figure 7.3 is an example of how I personally track our family receipts.

HSA Receipt Tracker				
Item	**Family Member**	**Date**	**Cost**	**Email Receipt**
Logan Walgreen's Medicine	Logan	1/19/23	$ 83.82	Yes
Sami Cam	Logan	2/4/23	$ 1,329.00	Yes
Logan Walgreen's Medicine	Logan	3/25/23	$ 31.39	Yes
Logan Walgreen's Medicine	Logan	3/29/23	$ 6.79	Yes
Logan Walgreen's Medicine	Logan	4/28/23	$ 8.26	Yes
Erin OB	Erin	4/27/23	$ 336.31	Yes
Logan Walgreen's Medicine	Logan	6/2/23	$ 12.67	Yes
Erin US	Erin	6/28/23	$ 137.36	Yes
Logan Keto Machine	Logan	6/28/23	$ 97.40	Yes
2023 Total			**$ 2,043.00**	

Figure 7.3 HSA receipt tracker.

Action Plan: Start Growing Your Money: Invest Now

Start investing today. Don't stress over how much to invest, thinking you have to invest some impressive amount. You can begin with a low amount or even invest relatively small amounts each month. The key is to start. Remember the beauty of compound interest plays on the idea of time. It is also important for you to think about the different types of investments and which are right for you. Even just $500 per month for 40 years at historical market returns will yield $2,655,555.

Step #1: Use the six-step process outlined in Lesson 7 to start investing.

Step #2: As you pick your investments, remember that it is best to invest in things you know and understand.

Step #3: Set up dollar cost averaging, which automates everything for you. This prevents you from trying to time the market or forget to invest. You select the investment, the investment amount, and time for those investment payments to come out of your account and into the investment account or plan.

Step #4: Whatever you choose to invest in, buy it and hold it. Don't try to time the market; it is a costly mistake.

Step #5: Use a compound interest calculator to see how much your current investing strategy is projected to yield in the future if you continue. You can access an investor calculator provided by the U.S. Securities and Exchange Commission at Investor.gov. I also added a direct link in the Resources at the end of the book for easy access.

At this point on your journey, you should be feeling pretty excited and more at ease. You are on your way to building wealth and achieving your goals and dreams. Being strategic, disciplined, and having a plan has brought you this far. Let's continue the journey.

Part III

Protect Your Money

Chapter 8
Build Your Moat

A sad reality of life is that many people, including the affluent, who have or have had stellar careers and have amassed a good fortune, don't always protect their money. They make costly mistakes that catch up with them in the end. Like everything that we have been discussing, it comes down to planning, which includes plans to protect your money after building it. In this part of your financial journey, you still need to be consistent, as we have discussed throughout the book, which includes establishing good habits and routines and consistency with your finances.

We all know that unexpected things happen. People often quip "life happens." Intellectually, we understand this idea, but emotionally we dismiss it as if that will keep accidents, illnesses, crises, and death away from us. Well, it won't. In fact, not planning and not being prepared for these things will only make things worse. I know from first-hand experience through my daughter's diagnosis of Dravet Syndrome that unexpected things happen, hence the word unexpected. So, in order to handle the unexpected, at least financially, you must plan for it.

There are a variety of things and means by which to prepare for the future and protect your money. By growing your money, there is an inherent risk of loss. Hopefully, you will be that rare individual for whom life will always go as planned and you will never face adversity or any calamity. Or you may be the person who faces a life situation or even a dire situation that is less catastrophic because you were prepared. This will happen IF you plan accordingly and sooner rather than later.

Lesson 1: Protecting Your Money Through Insurance

The first thing you need to do is make sure you have all of the necessary insurances. I don't advocate being over-insured, nor do I espouse using insurance as a savings account. That is the purpose of your investments. But you do need to make sure that you have ample insurance to safeguard against the unexpected. There are a variety of insurances that you can use for protecting yourself. The main ones I will focus on as being the most important are: auto, life, health including vision and dental plans, homeowners/renters insurance, long-term disability, long-term care for those over 55, umbrella insurance, and ID theft insurance.

Home, car, and health insurance are the ones that most people typically have. Home insurance is not state-mandated, but it is usually required by the mortgage lender, so we don't really get an option whether or not to purchase it. Car insurance is mandatory in all states except for New Hampshire, so that is the catalyst to purchase it. Even in New Hampshire, while it is not mandatory, drivers who do not have insurance must meet certain financial requirements.

An insurance broker who shops around for the lowest rates without sacrificing coverage is always the best move. You can always use a local insurance broker. If you don't have an insurance broker, here is what I would do to begin that search. I believe checking in with friends and family regarding a good contact is always your best bet. Word-of-mouth referrals seem to have the best results. If you do not have any word-of-mouth referrals, Google search local insurance brokers. Request a quote from various brokers and find who you want to work with the most.

Regarding insurance in general, while each has its place in helping you protect your money, I'd say the most essential type of insurance is life insurance. There are many life insurance options out
there, but I can say with certainty that a simple term life insurance
policy through a trusted broker is the best move 99.99% of the time.
I explain why below. Right now, let's look at the eight types of insurance noted above, so you have a good understanding of each as well
as your personal needs.

Auto Insurance

This insurance is one that most people are familiar with and typically have since it is illegal in almost all states not to have it if you
own a vehicle. According to *Forbes Advisor*, "the average cost of
car insurance is $2,150 for full coverage and $467 for state minimum coverage" (Gusner, 2023), but that is far lower than the cost
when you are involved in a car accident. Rates are based on criteria
including things such as your age, driving record, the type of coverage, the amount of the deductible, the make, model, and year of
the car, the state in which the vehicle is registered, and even your
credit history, which is yet another reason to be aware of your credit
history. I recommend shopping around to get comparative rates for
this insurance and to be aware of what your policy covers and does
not cover. You can use one of the links above to get a rate for car
insurance. Definitely do not go without coverage.

Life Insurance

To help protect your money and secure the lives of your loved ones, you
need life insurance. It is not mandatory according to state or federal
laws, and is one that nobody wants to discuss as if it will cause something terrible to immediately happen. But life insurance is paramount.
Here is a caveat. If, and only if, you have enough money in investments and savings that in the event of your death your loved ones
would be financially secure and would not have to depend on your
income to live as they had been when you were alive, then you do not

have to have life insurance. Remember the purpose of life insurance is to protect your family upon your death. So, if your family depends on you, you need life insurance. Typically, you want to have 10–12 times your salary for your insurance policy value. For example, if your salary is $100,000, you would need between $1 to $1.2 million dollars of life insurance. The thought is that if the insured dies, the insurance money will be invested and would get a return of 8–10%, which would replace the lost salary. Perhaps you will have enough money that your loved ones will be financially secure if and when something happens to you. But until that time occurs, you need life insurance.

When it comes to life insurance, there are two basic types to consider: term life insurance and permanent life insurance. There are some vast differences to consider when deciding between the different types. Term life insurance lasts only for a specified term while permanent life insurance lasts for your entire lifespan as long as you are paying your premiums. Another difference is the cost. Generally, term life insurance is relatively affordable and is dependent upon the term or number of years that you specify such as one, ten, or thirty. A downside to term life insurance is that it will expire at the end of the term. That may mean you need to renew the policy or write a new one.

Permanent life insurance, on the other hand, is less straightforward. You know I like simplicity, but this type of insurance is not simple. The complexity comes in with all of the fees, taxes, interest, and other costs and stipulations associated with it. One huge difference, and an aspect that some people like, is that there is a cash value with permanent life insurance. In addition, it is more costly than term life insurance, costing 5–15 times more.

Typically, I would not advise you to waste your money on permanent life insurance, at least for the vast majority of the population. Generally they are more expensive than term life insurance. In fact, permanent life insurance is about 5–15 times more expensive than term life insurance and is advertised as a hybrid investment/insurance account. You do not need a savings account or an investment fund in life insurance because you have already secured those in your financial plan. Please do not be lured into buying permanent life insurance. Find a good insurance agent whom you trust and get term life insurance until you no longer need it to financially secure your loved ones.

Health Insurance

Some people are lucky enough to have some or all of their health insurance covered by their employer. That is such a boon. If you fall into that category, congratulations! Consider yourself lucky. What a saving! If you are not, you should cover your health expenses with some type of insurance. There are a variety of plans available, from those that are expensive and have low deductibles all the way to less expensive plans that are meant mainly to cover more catastrophic illnesses and diagnoses and have high deductibles. Regardless of the plan you determine best for you, don't leave yourself or your family uninsured. Moreover, don't be tempted to go uninsured by the false notion that you are young, healthy, and/or have never had any real health issues. It is Murphy's Law just waiting to pounce!

There are five employer-provided health insurance types that you should understand:

1. **Exclusive Provider Organization (EPO) Plan:** This is a health insurance plan that provides insurance coverage as long as the healthcare providers are in the plan's network. The exception to this is in the event of an emergency. Going outside the network of healthcare providers is costly and typically not covered under the plan.
2. **Health Maintenance Organization (HMO):** An HMO is a plan similar to an EPO in that it also usually limits a person's medical coverage to care provided by medical professionals who work for or are in a contract with the insurance company and in facilities that are in the network of that HMO. HMOs often focus on maintenance, thus providing services that help promote wellness and prevent illnesses and diseases.
3. **Point of Service Plan (POS):** Similarly to HMOs and PPOs, with POS plans, you typically pay less if you use a care provider that is affiliated with the plan's network. Most of the time, this

type of plan requires a referral from a primary care provider for any kind of specialist. It is called a Point of Service plan because the insured has the option at each service facility to choose whether or not to stay with the associated healthcare providers. This also includes the types of services that are available based on the providers and the plan.

4. **Preferred Provider Organization (PPO):** PPO plans are quite similar to POS plans such as typically paying less for all of the care providers within the plan's network and paying an additional cost for those outside the network of the healthcare providers and facilities. But a major difference is that with a PPO plan, you don't typically need to have a referral.

5. **High Deductible Health Plan (HDHP):** HDHP plans, as noted by the name of the plan, have a higher deductible than traditional plans. However, with HDHP plans, the insured usually pays more for services provided before the insurance begins to cover the cost of the healthcare services.

Dental and vision insurance fall under this same category as health insurance. They also are not mandatory but can help save money, thus protecting your money. Definitely they are well worth costing out. For example, if you wear glasses and know that you will need yearly visits to the optometrist, having vision insurance often outweighs the cost of the examination, diagnosis, and treatment as well as the cost of glasses and contacts. Think beyond the basics, which can include needing to see an ophthalmologist. Those visits and procedures can be very costly. Do your homework and make sure the insurance is worth it as a means to offset the costs and, importantly, will actually cover the procedure.

Treat dental insurance the same as vision insurance. Assess where you are and what your personal oral health is. For us, this was worth the cost since both of us have two visits per year, which can include X-rays, cleanings, and fluoride treatments. Do the math first and get some competitive quotes. This insurance can be especially important if you don't have good oral health and need more extensive dental work completed. Don't waste your money; that is the key.

Homeowners Insurance and Renters Insurance

Don't discount protecting your home, your belongings, and even yourself by thinking you don't need this type of insurance, won't use it, or will save money by not purchasing it. Work with a good broker to cover you for what you own. Having insurance to cover you in the event of a water leak or break, fire, and even theft is another way to protect your money. These repairs and replacements are usually pretty costly. If you own your home, usually it is a nominal amount for homeowners insurance. If you rent, this type of insurance covers your personal property but not the actual structure of the building. That is secured by your landlord. My advice is to get it, no doubt, but also to know what your policy covers. Make sure you list your possessions, even taking pictures, in the event that you must file a claim.

A standard homeowners policy includes four key aspects of coverage: the actual dwelling and other structures not included with the dwelling, such as a barn or a detached garage, personal property, and liability. Renters insurance covers personal property/possession, liability, and any additional living expenses incurred due to the accident.

Typically, a homeowners policy does not include flood insurance, hurricane insurance, or earthquake insurance. You definitely will want to consider your personal situation and area to determine whether any of these would be important for you to add to your policy.

Long-term Disability Insurance

Another way to protect your money and yourself is through long-term disability insurance. This type of insurance replaces your income in the event that you are unable to work due to an illness or an injury. It protects you and your family from eating up your savings and investments due to the loss of your wages. This insurance is not like health insurance, which pays doctor and medical bills for treatments, surgeries, and therapies. Rather think of this as a supplement to your lost income.

Typically, it doesn't pay 100% of your income unless that is the plan you prefer, but it is certainly an important layer of protection. Anyone who is dependent upon his or her income as a means of paying living expenses should consider purchasing long-term disability insurance.

Unfortunately, this insurance is rarely discussed and often overlooked. When considering this type of insurance, it should be between 60–70% of your gross income if you pay the premiums, which means there would be no taxes. However, if your employer pays the premium, the distributions are taxable. Therefore, you need 100% coverage since it is taxed.

Long-Term Care Insurance for Those 55 Years of Age or Older

Like long-term disability insurance, another insurance to consider, depending on how you structure your financial plan, is long-term care insurance for those who are 55 years of age or older. Whether we like to think about it or not, the reality is that all of us age and one day will be seniors. The good news is that people are living longer and healthier lifestyles today compared to years ago. But we also know that assisted living and senior living expenses are not cheap.

I was amazed at the cost of these facilities when my family was faced with having to put my maternal grandmother into an assisted living facility due to her suffering from advanced Parkinson's disease, which had become so severe that my grandfather and my mom could no longer provide adequate care for her.

All too quickly a person's life savings and investments can dwindle and disappear trying to pay for such care. That is the purpose of long-term care insurance. It is there to help defray some of the cost of the care for the aging and/or disabled. This can include care in their own homes or in a facility. This insurance is not relatively cheap, but it is less expensive than the cost of the care, especially if that care means the person has to be put into a care facility like my grandmother.

The cost is tied to a person's age, gender, and health. This is where planning comes into play again. How deep is your moat? What are your long-term financial goals and planning like? You need to protect your money, so having no plan for these things, which are inevitable, is NOT a plan.

Umbrella Insurance

Umbrella insurance is not something many people consider, but it is well worth having. It is insurance that provides an extra layer of protection for your assets. Think of it as insurance for the amount of your assets that is not covered by regular insurance. It protects the insured in lawsuits, injury to other people, and damage to other people's property. A downside is that it is not a standalone policy. You must have an existing homeowners policy in order to purchase umbrella insurance. If you have over $500,000 in assets, I highly recommend you add this insurance. A good rule to use when getting umbrella insurance is to cover yourself up to your net worth in order to have ample protection.

Identity Theft Protection

One other layer of protection, while it is not really an "insurance" such as the other plans, but is often overlooked, is identity theft protection. Please do not be foolish to think that this will never happen to you or that nobody will prey on you. According to the FBI, in 2022, the cost due to identity theft was $10.3 billion, which was up from 2021 when the cost was $6.9 billion (Federal Bureau of Investigation, 2022). None of us are insulated from this happening. It can be catastrophic and life-shattering. Additionally, it can also take an exorbitant amount of time dealing with all of the institutions necessary to secure new and correct documents.

We are all on our phones, computers, and other devices. Our information is out there. Do not make it easy for these thieves and scammers. Obviously there are things to do to protect yourself from identity theft, but it is not enough on its own. Personally, I use Zander Insurance to protect my identity and financial accounts. There are many good programs for you to buy, but you need to take the time and make the investment to protect yourself and your assets.

Overall, having these insurances will protect your money. Whether it is insurance to protect you in the event of an accident, homeowners insurance to protect your home in case of something unforeseen, health insurance for catastrophic illnesses like we have with Logan, or life insurance to protect your family if you die, it is paramount to have the right things in place, so you do not have to liquidate assets and savings to pay for the unexpected, which actually is fairly expected at some time or another. Usually it is not a matter of if something will happen but when it will happen.

Action Plan: Begin to Build Your Moat Through Insurance

Step #1: Using the following checklist, check the insurances that you do NOT have but need in order to protect yourself, your family, and your money. If you already have all of the necessary insurance, skip to Step #3.

_____ Auto Insurance
_____ Life Insurance
_____ Health Insurance
_____ Dental/Vision Insurance
_____ Homeowners/Renters Insurance
_____ Long-term Disability Insurance
_____ Long-term Care Insurance
_____ Umbrella Insurance
_____ Identity Theft Protection

Step #2: Find a good broker for your insurance needs. This is someone with whom you connect and trust. This is business so you want to make sure your needs are met without overpaying. Yes, your broker needs to make money, but not at your expense. Use the links from earlier in the chapter if you need to meet with an insurance broker or need to apply for insurance.

Step #3: Re-evaluate your insurance on a yearly basis to make sure your current needs are still adequately covered. Ask your underwriter or broker to compare prices to see if you can save money.

Step #4: Ask your insurance provider about prepaying your insurance policies. This can often result in savings on your annual premium.

Lesson 2: Protecting Your Money Through Tax Diversification

Tax diversification is also important as a means of protecting your money. Project 10, 20, 30, or more years into the future. Imagine working your financial plan all of those years, amassing a sizable and comfortable amount of money, only to lose it through hefty taxes. You don't want your retirement years filled with strife knowing that you have to pay taxes on the money that you saved all of those years. Again, it comes down to planning.

Tax diversification is part of that plan. It enables you to pay some of the money ahead of time and other money when you actually withdraw money from your investments. By diversifying, it helps you save money in the end. An example of this is investing some money in a Roth IRA whereby you pay the taxes upfront and also in a 401(k) on which you will get taxed when you withdraw. Paying some earlier and some later spreads out your taxes, helping you save more of your money overall. The goal is to find the sweet spot. Constantly evaluate and ultimately pay the least amount of taxes during your lifetime, which can be the biggest expense for many people.

There are three primary tax buckets which are pre-tax, Roth, and taxable. Being able to use your free cash flow available from your budget to fill up these buckets in the correct amount is usually a six-figure decision. While your friend or crazy Aunt Sally tells you to fill up your 401(k) with the best of intentions, they are not CPAs and don't understand tax code. Neglecting tax optimization at this point can be a costly mistake.

Let's think of this in terms of dollars. What would happen if you lived to be a young 72 years of age and required minimum distributions (RMD) hit and all of your money was saved away in just a pre-tax 401(k). Is that the most ideal tax advantageous set-up? Probably not. There are ways to pull money from pre-tax up to the standard deduction tax-free, but you need to set yourself up to take advantage of that in your aging years. You can't fix what has already happened, but you can plan effectively NOW. If you are deliberate and intentional now, you will reap the benefits when you need the money to be there for you. So let's plan for that in this next lesson.

Lesson 3: Protecting Your Money Through Tax Planning and Tax Preparation

In order to know what investments are best for you, it is important to use the expertise of a tax planner. A tax planner will look at your financial picture, take into account your financial goals, and help you plan accordingly. Use the services of a tax planner to help protect your money and to avoid costly mistakes. Their purpose is different from a tax preparer. If you go to someone who prepares your taxes, generally that is all the person does.

Preparing taxes and possibly giving some general information or insight into your accounts and financial situation at that moment is totally different. It is not an encompassing thing and does not look at your entire financial situation. Protect what you have worked hard to grow by meeting with an accredited individual who will take the time to strategize for you. Your tax preparer may be able to perform that service, but it will be a different service than simply dropping off your W-2 to file your taxes. A candid conversation is warranted if that is the route you want to take.

Your best recourse is to use the services of a CPA. For tax planning, I suggest you meet with your CPA at least once a year and meet early to plan for the upcoming tax year. Tax planning entails assessing your situation to see how to best optimize your financial situation for the rest of the year such as paycheck adjustments and pre-tax versus post-tax retirement contributions and optimizing your tax buckets, as we just discussed in Lesson 2.

For tax preparation, I also recommend using the service of a good CPA. You should have a CPA file your taxes for that year. I advise you to do this at least in the first year to see if you have missed anything. Pay for the assurance that they are being completed correctly. It is well worth it and can save you from making costly mistakes. Going forward, if you have a basic tax situation with a standard 1040 tax form and nothing has changed year-from-year, you likely can replicate everything yourself using a service like TurboTax if you feel comfortable doing that.

Despite the fact that I am a CPA, I use a CPA because filing my taxes is not worth my time or the hassle that goes into it. Also, I like the extra feeling of security that my taxes are completed correctly due to all of the various and ever-changing tax codes and laws.

Action Plan: Protecting Your Money Through Tax Diversification, Tax Planning, and Tax Preparation

Step #1: Make an appointment to meet with a CPA or tax planner to plan ahead for the year for tax diversification and tax planning.

Step #2: Find a CPA to prepare and file your yearly taxes.

Lesson 4: Protecting Your Money Through Wills and Trusts

While similar, both acting to help protect your assets and carry out your wishes upon your death or incapacitation, wills and trusts are not the same thing. Both have benefits and certain uses and neither should be discounted as unnecessary. Each is meant to protect your assets, so we think of these as providing that layer of protection for our assets.

When we talk about wills, we are thinking about a legal document that distributes your assets to your heirs and beneficiaries after your death. Specifically, a will stipulates the wishes of a person regarding how his or her property will be distributed to his or her beneficiaries after death or in the event that the person cannot make decisions for himself or herself, along with who will manage the property until its final distribution.

In a will, you appoint who you wish to be the executor of your estate and some wills even stipulate funeral and burial wishes. Wills can also appoint a trustee who is in charge of the assets for minors until the stipulated age, as noted in the will, if that is a consideration.

Because it is a legal document, wills must be signed and witnessed as required by state law. Wills must follow a legal process upon the death of the testator (the person making the will). The will must be filed in probate court in the testator's jurisdiction. Wills are to be carried out according to the wishes of the testator by the designated executor of the will. They are considered public records in the probate court in which they were signed and filed. The probate court has jurisdiction over the execution of the will and oversees any disputes that may arise if the will is contested.

Trusts, on the other hand, are legal arrangements for the transfer of legal assets from the owner, called a grantor or a trustor, to the trustee. They set the terms for the trustee's management of the assets for distribution to one of more designated beneficiaries and for the disposition of the assets. Trustees are fiduciaries, meaning they are in charge of managing money and/or property for another person. As fiduciaries, the role of the trustee is to handle the assets of the grantor in accordance with the terms specified in the trust as well as in the best interest of the beneficiary or beneficiaries. Trusts do not take place upon the death of the grantor like a will does with the death of the testator but rather upon the transfer of assets to the beneficiary. Living trusts are an example of trusts created during the lifetime of the grantor. These are often used in estate planning and are created to benefit their heirs.

Both wills and trusts protect your money and safeguard your assets for your family. Wills and trusts are not contingent upon how much money you have. Everyone with dependents needs some type of will and/or trust as a plan for when they die, which is inevitable. If you do not have a will, the courts can decide what to do with your assets. This is known as being intestate.

Think about that for a moment. Imagine building up your wealth and assets but having no will. Upon your death, the probate court takes over your estate, whatever that entails, and will decide what will happen to all of your property and assets. Your estate becomes public record, which means information about your property, finances, and family is disclosed. Most people do not want this type of information made public. Since this is supervised by the courts, it also means the process can take months to even a year to settle the estate. The courts even have jurisdiction to decide what will happen to your children if they are minors when you die. This, of course, is handled according to the laws stipulated in your individual state.

From a financial perspective, trusts can provide tax efficiency because they are invisible to the IRS. This means the assets aren't reported as gains, losses, gift taxes, or income taxes on assets that are sold in a trust. Only income and revenue that is made from assets in a trust are subject to taxes. Trusts also allow distribution control since you do not have to distribute your assets outright but can customize it, transferring assets as you determine and when you determine.

Think about this as another layer of protection for your assets. This is a way to deepen your moat. When your estate is probated, all debtors and creditors must be notified so they can all make claims on your assets. When your assets are secured in a trust, it is not made public, so they are not notified. This protects your assets from being used to pay debts.

Lastly, it protects your family from having to pay expensive attorney fees. It is not easy or cheap to have to probate an estate, especially without the help of an attorney. The assets remain tied up until the estate is settled through the courts. Therefore, your heirs can't pay for the attorney with the assets until the estate is settled, so they have to pay the expenses themselves.

Bottom line, do not go without a will or a trust. The process is not complicated or expensive, but it will protect you so it is well worth the time and effort.

Action Plan: Strengthen Your Moat with Wills and Trusts

Step #1: You will need to decide to whom your assets will be given, either through a will or a trust. This can be one person, several people, or even organizations.

Step #2: What assets do you have to bequeath to this person, persons, or organization? Be as specific as possible.

Step #3: Who do you feel is the best person to handle your estate as the executor of your will or the trustee of your trust? Keep in mind that this individual must be someone you trust to carry out all of your wishes as specified.

Step #4: Find an estate planner or an attorney to draw up your will or trust. Remember, these are legal documents, so it is best to get a professional who handles these specifically to safeguard you in the long run.

Lesson 5: Protecting Your Money Through Durable Powers of Attorney

When setting up wills and trusts, you also have the option to choose a durable healthcare power of attorney and financial power of attorney. This may sound complicated, but I assure you it is not. These two documents simply give you the option to transfer power to someone else if you are unable to make healthcare or financial decisions. Some people feel that these are two of the most important documents each person over the age of 19 should have. Like wills and trusts, durable power of attorney documents safeguard you and your family and provide protection.

A durable power of attorney for healthcare also known as a healthcare power of attorney or healthcare POA is a legal document giving a trusted adult authority to make medical decisions for you if you are not able to express them yourself. This authority includes making end-of-life decisions. If you have a living will, the healthcare POA carries out your wishes as stipulated.

A financial power of attorney is also a legal document, in which you, the principal, give authority to an individual whom you trust, your agent, to manage your financial and legal affairs. The agent has your permission as such to manage your finances should you become incapacitated or unable to handle your affairs. The agent has authority to do things involving your finances such as pay bills and taxes, make investments on your behalf, transfer and sell assets, buy and handle insurance for you, and have access to all of your financial accounts, including your investments and retirement. Basically, the agent, appointed by you, will handle all of your affairs and act in your best interest. That is why it is imperative that you appoint someone you trust explicitly.

Durable powers of attorney is a step that people too often skip, which can have detrimental consequences. Do not leave yourself vulnerable and unprotected. This, like so much of what we have discussed, takes planning. But it is a huge mistake not to make the time to plan so you can secure your future and safeguard your loved ones.

Action Plan: Establish Your Durable Powers of Attorney

Step #1: The first step is to carefully choose one person whom you trust and who is responsible to act as your durable power of attorney. This is a person who will act in your best interest. It is usually best to only select one person, but you may want to also choose one backup person in the event that your first selection can't fulfill his or her duties.

(continued)

(*continued*)

Step #2: Fill out the correct form to stipulate exactly what you want your durable power of attorney to do. You can get generic forms online, but you must read them carefully to make sure they stipulate everything you want but don't include other clauses that are not part of your wishes. You can also see an attorney to complete the form.

Step #3: Have your form officially notarized. Most states require the form to be notarized. but do not require it to be filled. Check with your individual state for specifics.

Step #4: Make copies of the form, keep one for yourself, and give one to your durable power of attorney.

Lesson 6: Protecting Your Money Through Credit

I would be a bit remiss if I did not discuss credit, but I also need to say that I think credit is a bit overrated and overhyped. I know people get worried about credit scores and ratings, and we are also told how imperative they are for our purchasing powers. I don't put too much emphasis on credit alone because if you are actively doing everything you have been taught to this point, you will naturally have a great credit score. However, it is important to be educated on credit to ensure you are aware of the factors that drive your credit score.

Credit is broken down into five categories to create your Vantage score, which is your credit score. The categories are not equal percentages. Different categories comprise different percentages, totaling 100%. The categories from highest to lowest individual percent are payment history, 35%; amounts owed, 30%; length of credit history, 15%; credit mix, 10%; and new credit, 10%. Let's take a look at each category, so you can understand them fully to make sure you have a good credit score.

Payment history comprises the largest percentage of your Vantage score and shows that you have made your payments consistently in a timely manner. To ensure that you do that, automate. We have discussed this several times. Also, make sure you are paying the full balance billed, not just the minimum payment amount billed, to help with your overall credit score. Late and missed payments will be noted as derogatory marks on your credit report and will lower your credit score.

The second largest percentage is the amounts owed category, or the ratio of credit balance to your credit limit. It is recommended to keep the ratio under 30%, but keeping it lower is better. To calculate your percentage simply divide your balance amount by your limit. For example, if I have a $1,000 limit, and I have a balance of $200, my ratio is 20%. To boost your credit score, make sure your usage is below 10%. You can also improve this category by making credit card payments throughout the month, so you never have your usage increase. Another thing you can do to improve in this category is to request a credit card increase. Keep your spending the same, but the ratio to spend or the usage will be far less as a percentage. Your credit score will increase dramatically as a result. Just be careful not to start spending extra just because you have a higher limit. Don't use it just because you have it, but if you do use it, watch your ratio.

Your credit history is 15% of your score. The longer you have had a credit history, the higher your score, provided you have established a good history. Five years of good history is considered an average credit history, seven years is great, and nine or more is excellent. To boost your score, start building credit earlier rather than later. You can add your child as an authorized user on your credit card as a way to build a credit history for him or her. My wife's parents did this for her, establishing her credit when she was about 16. You need to check with your credit card company because each one has different rules about minors.

The fourth and fifth categories, credit mix, which is 10%, and new credit, also 10%, are coupled. These categories are simply the different types of loans you have and new loans you open. Credit card companies need to see that you are able to make your payments on time and that you are also able to make a variety of payments. It is good to have several different types of loans such as a mortgage and a credit card, but you do not want to have too many and/or not be able to make your payments.

Regarding your credit overall, you want to ensure that you don't have anything that detracts from your credit that can negatively impact your credit score. This could include missed payments or delinquent accounts, owing too many creditors, or even a lack of credit. Additionally, you will want to ensure you do not have any derogatory marks and minimal credit inquiries. Credit inquiries will negatively impact your credit history.

There are two different types of credit pulls that you should understand. There are soft pulls, which means you have given someone permission to check your credit report. This does not impact your credit score. This would be something you would do for a preapproved credit card or for loans. Hard pulls, on the other hand, do show up on your credit report. Hard pulls mean you have given permission to someone to view your credit report, so you can get approved for a new line of credit. These have a low impact on your Vantage score, but too many of them over a short period of time is not good. These stay on your credit report for two years and typically affect your credit report for about a year.

You NEVER want derogatory marks on your credit report as they are a negative indication of your poor credit activity, such as late payments, accounts in collection, debt settlements, foreclosures, or tax liens. These stay on your credit report for 7–10 years. In some cases, they can even stay indefinitely.

There are strategies to remove the derogatory marks on your credit report. One is to submit a dispute to the credit bureau. Second, you can submit a dispute with the business reporting to the credit bureau.

For credit in general, I highly recommend checking your credit report once a year. Be careful that you do NOT check it more than once per year or it will adversely impact your score. More is not better here. The goals are obviously to see what your credit score is and to make sure there are no negative marks. In addition, check your credit report to ensure there is no identity theft or cyber criminals opening lines of credit in your name. There are free ways to get your credit report at three credit bureaus which are Experian,

Transunion, and Equifax. To do this, go to `AnnualCreditReport.com` at `https://www.annualcreditreport.com/index.action`.

Ultimately, you want a credit score of 740 or higher. A credit score of 740 and higher will generally provide you with all of the benefits you can achieve, such as a lower mortgage interest rate, car loan interest rate or easier approval by landlords. Anything above this has diminishing returns, if any. I would not stress about your credit score over and above 740. A score of 850 is the highest credit score possible in both the FICO and the VantageScore credit scoring systems. One way to track your credit score is through Credit Karma. I have the Credit Karma app on my phone, and I generally check my credit score once per month.

Action Plan: Check Your Credit

Step #1: Download the Credit Karma app and check your credit score (monthly).

Step #2: Check your Credit Report at `AnnualCreditReport.com` (annually).

Step #3: Set a Google reminder to check your credit report one year from the date that you last checked it. Remember, this should be annually but should not be more than once a year.

Overall, all of these insurances are key to you protecting yourself, your family, and your assets. These are easy ways for you to build your moat. Most of them do not even take that much time. Invest the time and money now to protect your money. If you put these things off, it may be too late. Seriously, not having these layers of protection in place can be devastating and can have dire consequences. Don't be in the situation where you say you wish you would have or you should have done any of these things. I have often reminded you that life happens. We all know it does, so prepare for it today. If you did not complete any of the action plans for Chapter 7 and this chapter, now is the time to go back and complete them.

Chapter 9

Budgetdog, My Money Mindset, and My Passion

You have put in the commitment of time and effort to this point and have learned the pillars of the Budgetdog Framework. Congratulations! But don't celebrate too fast. This final piece is the single most important topic you will learn about. It is your money mindset. We talked about the psychology behind money, so you know your unconscious mind rules your money behavior, whether that is spending, saving, or investing. Your unconscious largely controls your behavior and emotions in general. So, you need to have a good money mindset in order to stick to the plan. When you do that, our financial goals will come to fruition.

But the key is **awareness**. Once you become aware, I mean truly cognizant, you are able to pre-plan actions before situations and feelings arise, especially the negative ones that lead to lapses in desired behaviors. For example, if you have a feeling you are going to stress-buy, you need to have a pre-planned goal to do something in lieu of going to the mall, such as taking a walk or going to the gym.

Having a money mindset will enable you to continue to stick to the plan. That is one of the reasons that I want you to automate everything along the way. We all are human, which means we are fallible and often lapse back into bad habits or even become complacent. Let's face it. Sometimes life just happens, things get hectic, and before too long the day is over and the week is over and we have forgotten to pay the bills, go to the gym, put money into investments, and the list goes on and on. That is real. I get it. Automating is one way to ensure long-term success. It eliminates one variable that could cause us to fail. Between automating and being intentional with your money mindset, you will create a sustainable model that works for you for the rest of your life.

Another important aspect is to make sure you are really in tune with who you are. There are a host of personality tests that you can take to assess this, such as the Myers-Briggs Type Indicator. This test, for example, assesses 16 different types of personalities from a variety of questions. It assesses things from whether or not you are an introvert or an extravert, which is basically where you are most comfortable in your world and the world around you, to how you make decisions as a thinking or feeling type of person. Thinking individuals generally look at logic and reason things out, compared to feeling individuals who consider people and circumstances when trying to make decisions. Understanding your personality, what motivates you, and your triggers is important for goal-setting. Remember in Chapter 2, Lesson 5, we discussed the fact that around 92% of the population will fail in their goals. Understanding who you are can better enable you to achieve your goals. The key point here is to be fully aware of yourself, cognitively, in order to successfully continue on the financial plan you have put in place.

Action Plan: Identify Your Personality: Know Yourself

Step #1: Take the Myers-Briggs Type Indicator test or a similar test.
Myers-Briggs online at: https://www.mbtionline.com/?utm_source=MBF&utm_medium=link&utm_campaign=online
or take the Typefinder Personality Test online at: https://www.truity.com/test/type-finder-personality-test-short.

> **Step #2:** Analyze your results to gain a better understanding of your personality.
>
> **Step #3:** Using what you have learned from this, write down your triggers and pre-plan, so you are better equipped to prevent failures or things that will prevent you from staying on track and reaching your goals.

Being self-aware, not only of your strengths but also your weakness, can have a fundamental impact on success. Believe me, I am quite aware of my weaknesses, of which I have several, or, based on who you are talking to, such as my wife when she thinks I am not listening to her, maybe even many! But my self-awareness has helped me and even really shaped me. For example, I have always believed I would build a business that helps millions. The entrepreneur in me knew I would create something but, for a long time, I didn't fully know what it would be or how it would come to fruition. Nonetheless, I always believed and searched.

This insight helped me create the idea for my business, step-by-step on my laptop while sitting in a McDonald's parking lot. When I showed it to Erin, I told her this was the biggest thing I have done to date and that it was going to be hugely successful. Of course, we couldn't confirm it at the time, but I was sure I was right.

But again, being self-aware and transparent here as to who I am and my personality type, the thinking personality that I am, according to the Myers-Briggs Type Indicator test, prevented me initially from taking the leap of faith I needed when I did begin to carve out my vision. Because I am a thinking type of person, looking at things logically and consistently, I remained stuck in the corporate world. It made sense. It was logical or so it seemed for a while. I had a wife, a mortgage, and responsibilities. We were paying the bills and living like all of our friends. Why would I leave any of that? I couldn't. That is what you have to understand. What type of person are you and is that helping you or hurting you? In many cases, it has served me well. Now, it was not playing in my favor.

It actually was my wife, Erin, typically and in personality not as much of a logical, thinking person as I am, who convinced me to start my own business that transformed into what Budgetdog is today. She leans more to being a feeling type, according to the Myers-Briggs Type Indicator test. But she could see how what I was describing to her could be a game-changer for us. Oh, we had many, many late-night discussions on our back porch talking about and honing the idea of Budgetdog. Her faith in me and my vision gave me the confidence to begin. Me, being hyper-logical at times, decided to begin small, keep my corporate job at Deloitte, and assess accordingly.

These discussions, of which we had too many to count, led me to create an Instagram account on my week off. At the time, I had no clue what I was doing or how to start a business. I didn't even have the full vision of how far the business would ultimately go. All I really had was my conviction. I knew where we were headed and how far we had come. If we could be successful, reaching our goals to pay off our debts in such a short period of time and be on our way to becoming millionaires at such a young age, and if my friends and acquaintances who I was helping could be successful on their financial journey, then I knew others could be too. I wanted to reach all of you who were beyond my reach unless I made my message viral. So I took that leap and wrote my first Instagram post on the steps of a church, naming my Instagram account and now company after my dog Niko.

My message about all of this is to know yourself and find your passion. Keep your money mindset and you will also see success. My goals and success aren't the same as your goals and idea of success. Think about all of the different personalities noted in the personality profiles. We are all vastly and uniquely different. Coupled with that is our money value system that we discussed in Chapter 2. Building my company has taken time and help along the way. Just as I am mentoring you on your journey, I had fantastic mentors who helped me get started and, more importantly, continue to help me keep going. Without the help of mentors and a support group, many of us will fail.

Outside of Erin, who brought her own clarity, vision, and artistic talent to Budgetdog, two key mentors who guided me and kept me going on my trajectory upward are Chris Johnson, creator of The Wealth Squad, and Sean Cranston, The Wealth Dad. Both Chris and Sean are highly successful entrepreneurs. Reaching out to them and using their innovative business models while adding my own personal twist, have helped me continue to grow Budgetdog and to be able to appeal to a broader and larger audience. Their mentorship and friendship are invaluable to me.

I am following in the footsteps of tremendous minds and amazing people. They are revolutionary in their areas, breaking barriers and reaching beyond what can only be imagined. It is not about the money. Owning my own company has allowed me the lifestyle I only envisioned. It has enabled Erin and me to be able to quit our 9-to-5 jobs and live a life free from the restrictions that were placed on us through those jobs. For us, that did not fit any longer. But what I am doing now with Budgetdog is not the right fit for everyone either. Being the owner of an online platform is not without commitment, time, and energy. It is just different because I play on my terms now and by my rules. This has helped me grow as a person. It has opened up many new opportunities for me and for my family. Remember, we discussed the importance of discovering your WHY. Providing for my family and giving them the life they need, especially Logan, is my ultimate goal.

My journey has helped me reach millionaire status by the age of 30. How? Vision. I stayed true to my convictions and belief in what I was doing. Don't listen to those who criticize what you are doing as being nonsensical or too idealistic. Follow your dreams and your goals. I don't give credence to those who make fun of others who chase their dreams.

If we all stopped chasing our dreams, where would we be? Think about great visionaries and inventors. They don't all need to be people who changed the world, just founders and those who had a vision such as Ray Kroc.

Kroc, originally a somewhat unsuccessful traveling salesman, stopped at a hamburger joint in California on his travels when trying to sell Multimixers. The restaurant was owned by two brothers, Richard and Maurice McDonald, and it ran with precision and efficiency like no other restaurant that Kroc had experienced. Kroc's vision was to take that business model and franchise it, which he did. Think about how many McDonald's there are today, all following the same basic business model as the original McDonald's in 1954. Tens of thousands around the world. That is vision. It is the same vision as Travis Kalanick, founder of Uber, and Mark Zuckerberg, cofounder and CEO of Facebook. I am sure in the earliest phases of all visionaries' journeys, there is ridicule and perhaps even condemnation. Don't be dissuaded as long as it is practical and there is a true vision. Just make sure you're ready to experience difficulties, setbacks, and bumps along the way.

I didn't listen or give credence to what others were saying or to any of their disparaging remarks. Because of that, I have been featured in publications and on podcasts, and I am taking my business nationwide. Ironically, Budgetdog Academy came together on the steps of a McDonald's. Go figure!

What I want for you is for you to continue to soar. Reach your goals and your WHY, stay the course, and change your life by becoming financially independent. It will change your outlook, perspective, and psyche. I will continue to be your mentor. Lean on me for help and guidance at @Budgetdog.

Chapter 10

Logan Lee, an Unimaginable Reality: My WHY

This chapter drills down to my WHY, specifically, and what keeps me pushing to exceed my financial goals as well as how having a plan, at least a solid financial plan, is imperative. Here is where the chaos and unpredictability came into play in my life. It is all about my family, especially my daughter Logan. That does not mean I love one of my daughters more than another or the other one less. As a parent, you know you love all of your children equally but differently. But it is truly Logan who was the catalyst behind us being not only financially independent but also financially well off enough to afford the type of care that Logan needs.

I know I am not the only one who has a child or family member who has special medical needs. I also know that there are many who have situations far worse and far more devastating than mine. As our lives have taken a different path than what we expected and hoped when Erin was pregnant, we have heard countless stories of tragic situations that are beyond comprehension and ones I can never even imagine having to endure.

But for me, I have to deal with the situation that I am facing. As a father, I often feel helpless. I am not a doctor or one of Logan's many specialists who know what to do to help her. So beyond loving Logan more than I can even begin to describe on paper, the only thing I can do to help her is to be able to put her in the right place with the best healthcare specialists possible. Let me explain and introduce you to Logan and her story.

Her story is real life. It is our "normal" now and has changed our lives in ways that are unimaginable. This was unpredictable, as life usually is. That is what I want you to be ready for. I never thought the real world would come my way, but it did. Keep in mind that in today's world of Facebook, Instagram, etc., we often live behind a façade that is touched up and false. This is not a retouched, sugar-coated picture of my life.

I am going to step back first to say that before January 29, 2022, my life was very satisfying. I was happy. At that time I was, by all definitions, financially, personally, and professionally fairly successful. Life was good for my wife and me as a married couple building our lives together and building a family. On September 4, 2021, we were blessed with our beautiful daughter, Logan. Things couldn't seem to get much better. At that same time, I was building Budgetdog, had quit Deloitte, so I was able to stay at home to care for Logan, which was a blessing.

Then life happened! It is the part you never really plan for emotionally. On January 29, 2022, our whole world was turned upside down and inside out. The life we had came to an abrupt and screeching halt. On that tragic day, our baby who we thought was healthy, suffered her first seizure. It was a harrowing experience.

Imagine my panic when Erin came running hysterically into the room where I was preparing to make a company presentation, shaking and saying that something was terribly wrong with our baby. As most who suffer some type of shocking event or trauma, I still can remember every minute detail from that experience and relive it over and over in slow motion.

After arriving at the emergency room and having Logan evaluated, we were reassured that babies having seizures is not that uncommon and were discharged. We left the hospital, feeling somewhat better but still frightened only to return by ambulance exactly 24 hours later when Logan had another seizure. We kept wondering if this, too, was "normal" as our minds were a whirlwind of incoherent and jumbled thoughts. In the space of one day, our lives had changed forever.

That became our first of many hospital stays; it lasted four days but provided few answers. Questions plagued us and went unanswered. Finally, after a battery of tests, they were ready to discharge us with little information other than things seemed to be okay now. As we were preparing to leave, a doctor came back in, telling us they noticed something on the EEGs that did not seem "right." What did that even mean? We were sickened by so many medical terms, so many questions, and so many incoherent thoughts that we were trying to absorb.

Since that fateful day, we have had too many ambulance runs to the ER and too many hospital stays. For context, in 2022 alone, we had 18 ER visits,11 extended hospital stays, two visits to Texas for special care, and over $200,000 in medical bills. By the eighth full month into that year alone, our total hospital bills soared past $150,000. By then we also had come to know too many of the amazing nurses in the Neurology unit at Cincinnati Children's Hospital and the EMTs who all knew the drill too well when they got the frequent 911 calls to our house.

Eventually, after pushing and some thoughts, meeting somewhat fortuitously and serendipitously with seizure disorder specialists, in particular Dr. Perry in Texas, who was following me at Budgetdog at the time, we finally learned that Logan has Dravet Syndrome. In one fell swoop, our daughter, who appeared to be perfectly healthy, in less than one year was diagnosed with this rare syndrome that affects one in every 15,700 children. Like all syndromes, it presents itself differently in each child. Some children have mild and even few seizures, complications, and side effects, but others have many severe seizures and complications, including lags or regression in mental and physical development and even death in extreme cases, which is about 15–20% of those diagnosed with Dravet Syndrome. There is currently no cure for Dravet Syndrome. There is active research in the field and doctors are aware of the exact gene that is the main cause (SCN1A). We are hopeful that with time and more research, more questions will be answered and a cure will be discovered.

That is in the future, but it does not remedy the condition or situation for Logan now. We still have so many questions and no answers or guarantees. But isn't that all part of living in the real world?

Logan's constant monitoring is a reality; it is our responsibility and our lives. The more we can lessen the seizures, the better it is for Logan. Watching your child go through something like this is crushingly painful. Many of you know from first-hand experience what I am saying.

Being able to stay home with Logan has been a blessing. Budgetdog has enabled me to be there with her to monitor as many of the activities and situations as possible. The financial freedom that we have also enabled us to seize an opportunity to move from Kentucky to be closer to a new, state-of-the-art facility created just for seizure disorders. Had we not been in that situation, we would have had to run all over from one specialist, therapist, and doctor to another. Now, at Cook Children's Jane and John Justin Neurosciences Center in Fort Worth, Texas, all of the healthcare providers on Logan's team are in one place. They all know her and her history.

I never would have been able to be present for all of her care and its demands if I had not quit my job. It was a decision that simply was serendipitous. But that is the point; we never can predict what will come our way. We don't know what the future holds for us, but we can be financially prepared so we can more easily and on a different level deal with life as it happens.

I can't imagine trying to handle the stress of a financial worry on top of all of the anxiety we already have. Certainly I do not want anybody to have to deal with a situation like this. But it is real and unfortunately happens way too often. I can't tell you how to deal with such a devastating situation. The only advice I can give you is to make sure you don't leave yourself unprepared financially.

Every day we celebrate Logan where she is, and we know that she is *perfect* no matter what her perfect looks like. We are deeply committed to providing the best possible care we can for her, including the most up-to-date and effective medicines and therapies available. We have immersed ourselves in learning everything we can about Dravet Syndrome and are trying to bring awareness about it to everyone we can. In less than two short years, Logan has totally changed our lives. This is real. It is not always pretty or easy, but it is life as it is.

There have been many tears along the way, and we, in a sense, had to mourn the baby we thought we had. We could cry, but we chose to fight for Logan and all of the Logans out there.

For parents, there is no way to imagine loving a child any more than you do. Parents love their children unconditionally, wholeheartedly, and purely to a level that is like no other love. We know how blessed we are to be the parents of such an amazing daughter.

Logan has taught us how to be totally selfless and more appreciative for all of the blessings in life, as well as how not to take anything for granted. Living in the real world with Logan is unimaginably challenging but so remarkably rewarding and incredible. Every "normal" milestone for healthy children is catastrophic for Logan. Something as simplistic as cutting teeth brings about additional worries, even more careful monitoring, and upped medicines to offset seizures. She, and therefore we, are limited to exposure to other people, including our family, and to situations because they prove to be too much overstimulation for Logan, which can bring on her seizures. This means not being able to really celebrate holidays or even to have much of a get-together because they are too much for Logan. That is our reality and where we are right now. When my mother-in-law asked my father-in-law what he wanted for his birthday, his quick response was just to have Logan be able to hold his hand. We all pray for things like that. Maybe someday. Now you know my WHY.

Conclusion

Benjamin Franklin, statesman, visionary, and entrepreneur, said, "Little strokes fell great oaks"(Franklin, 2023). Keep that in mind. It is all of the little steps that we take that make a huge difference. We don't eat that elephant in one bite. Make a resolution to continue to make strides, step-by-step, little-by-little. You have taken lots of little steps to achieve something great—your goals. Each step is important, building on one another, and moving you step-by-step closer to your goal.

Throughout this book, we have talked about money and your relationship with it. You know you have to remember to plan for the occasions when you have negative experiences that can derail you from your financial goals. Together we have also worked through *tracking your money*, *growing your money*, and *protecting your money*, which are the three pillars of Budgetdog Academy. Make those things a priority. Like we discussed with NOW being the time for investing, NOW is also the time to make these positive changes in your life. Remember a key to financial success is automating—and maybe the whiteboard! Seriously, don't forget to put in place everything you can on automation, so you don't leave anything to chance.

Of course, as I have repeated many times, I can't overemphasize the importance of finding your passion and knowing your WHY. It is your driving force. It all begins with this. You have to know this and live this in order for you to be able to continue on your financial journey. Remember, it is not over. Yes, you have completed the steps and have changed your direction in a positive way. But now you must continue plugging away as you set each new goal. I challenge you to keep reassessing your situation and setting new goals. Reach beyond what you thought you could achieve. You can achieve whatever you want to accomplish. Bill Phillips, American entrepreneur and author of *Body for Life: 12 Weeks to Mental and Physical Strength* wrote: "The difference between who you are and who you want to be, is what you do" (Phillips, 2023). So what will you do? How will you continue on this journey? Where will you let yourself go?

It is not about money. This journey is about achieving the kind of freedom and life you want but only part of that picture includes your financial freedom. I told you my story with Logan, which is a huge part of my WHY. Yes, there is a component of that where money plays a part. It is important so we are able to afford the care she needs, having the moat around us so we don't meet with financial ruin due to her mounting medical bills or not having the money to be able to get all of her prescriptions. Of course, money is key. But making our journey also puts us in a position to be able to stay home with her to provide the monitoring and care she desperately needs. What is the price of that? Of course, it is priceless.

Having financial freedom and financial means also provides the luxury to give back. Our journey did not stop with paying off debt and creating Budgetdog. Now our journey means giving back to others, so they can achieve financial freedom along with contributing to research and institutions such as the Dravet Syndrome Foundation to whom the proceeds of this book will go. What a dream to be able to write them a check for a million dollars! Living a financially independent life has responsibilities to give to others. It is not a time to be selfish but a time to be selfless. That, too, is priceless.

Think about that. Think about being in a financial and life situation where you can selflessly and graciously serve the needs of others. That is a legacy. With all of the inventions that Benjamin Franklin had and all those upon which he improved, he never applied for a single patent or copyright. In his autobiography, Franklin wrote, "As we enjoy great advantages from the inventions of others, we should be glad of an opportunity to serve others by any invention of ours; and this we should do freely and generously." How will you serve others in this same spirit? How will you pay it forward and make the lives of others better?

You are off to your next journey now. I am always at your disposal and will remain your mentor along your path of life. You can message me directly at @Budgetdog via Instagram with your personal and more specific financial questions at any time. I look forward to hearing from each and every one of you. I want to hear your personal story and the path you have taken to achieve financial freedom and success. Let's meet at the top together!

Glossary of Common Investing Terms

401(k) A plan that is an employer-sponsored, tax-favored retirement savings account designed for the employees of the company.

403(b) A U.S. tax-advantaged retirement savings plan available for different organizations such as nonprofit employers, public school teachers, and some nonprofit employers.

457(b) A plan for firefighters, police officers, and other local government and state employees that is an employer-sponsored, tax-favored retirement savings account, also known as a deferred compensation plan.

529 College Savings Plan A 529 is a tax-advantaged investment plan designed to encourage saving for future education expenses for a person who is the designated beneficiary.

Amortization schedules This is the detailed listing of your debts including any student loans, car payments, and mortgage payments, the due date for each loan, the term of the loan, the total loan payment of each loan, and the interest rate for each.

Annual percentage rate (APR)   The annual percentage rate is the yearly rate you are charged for a loan or that you earn on an investment.

Asset classes   The five asset classes consist of cash and cash equivalents, stocks (equities), bonds (fixed income), real estate, and commodities (real assets).

Assets   These are the things that you own and include cash on hand, savings, investments, and tangibles that are owned.

Avalanche debt method   Using this method means you attack your debts in order of the interest rate rather than the debt amount, paying off those with the highest interest rate first and working through all your debts.

Balance sheet   Similar to your own balance sheet, it also can refer to a company's assets, liabilities, and shareholders' equity. It is the place where you list all assets and liabilities to see where you are.

Blend stocks   Stock that is a mix of growth stocks and value stocks.

Bond   This is the process of giving money to a company, corporation, or the government which is a loan from you to them when they want to raise money. In exchange, they generally agree to pay you a specified amount of interest. The most common types of bonds include municipal bonds and corporate bonds.

Brokerage fee   The fee the broker holding your investment account charges.

Budget   A budget is a detailed written plan that helps track your money, not intending to restrict you but rather to give you control over your money.

Budget billing   This is the tracking of 12 months of usage and then averaging that to provide you with that as your payment. Utility companies often offer this as a payment method. It allows you to better budget your expenses, turning them from variable to fixed.

Bull market   This is a market that is trending higher and likely to show a gain. If you think the market is going to go up, you are considered a "bull." If you are "bullish" about a specific company, it means you think the stock price will rise.

Capital gain or capital loss   This is the difference between what you paid for an investment and what you sold the investment for. For example, if you buy 100 shares of a stock at $10 a share, spending $1,000 altogether, and you sell your shares later for $25 a share totalling $2,500, you have a capital gain of $1,500. A loss occurs when you sell for less than you paid. So, if you sell this stock for $5 instead for a total of $500, you have a capital loss of $500.

Capital gains appreciation   The money earned from capital gains, which is taxed at different rates, depending on how long you hold the investment.

Commodities   These are products that consumers use, such as corn, wheat, or gas.

Common Stock Index Investment Fund (C Fund)   This fund is for those who are interested in a fund that attempts to match the outcomes and performance of the S&P 500 Index, thus providing the participant with equity ownership in midsize and large U.S. company stocks and offers the possibility of high investment returns over the long term.

Compound interest   The basic idea of this is that you are able to gain interest on the interest that your money earns over time. The longer you leave your money invested, the more it will grow exponentially; it continues to compound.

Diversification   A financial strategy that creates a mixture of different asset classes in a portfolio including stocks, bonds, real estate, and commodities.

Dividend   A dividend is a portion of a company's profit that is paid to common and preferred shareholders. Dividends provide an incentive to own stock in stable companies even if they are not experiencing much growth. Companies are not required to pay dividends.

Durable power of attorney   (Also known as a health care power of attorney or health care POA.) This is a legal document giving authority to a trusted adult to make medical decisions including end-of-life decisions for you in the event that you are not able to express them yourself.

Exchange fee   The cost or the fee that shareholders are charged if they exchange or transfer to a different fund that is within the same fund grouping.

Exchange-traded fund (ETF)   A type of investment fund that is traded on stock exchanges much like other securities.

Exclusive Provider Organization (EPO) Plan   This is a health insurance plan that provides insurance coverage as long as the health care providers are in the plan's network.

Executor or executrix   A man or woman respectively who has the sole responsibility of carrying out the wishes assigned to him or her through a will.

Expense ratio   An annual fee that all funds or exchange-traded funds (ETFs) charge their shareholders which includes 12b-1 fees, management fees, and plan administration fees.

Fiduciary   A person who is in charge of managing the money, property, or both of another person.

Financial power of attorney   A legal document giving a trusted adult authority to manage your financial and legal affairs if you become incapacitated or unable to handle your own affairs.

Fixed expenses   Expenses that stay the same from month to month, such as a car payment, student loan payment, and mortgage payment.

Fixed income   Income that does not vary from paycheck to paycheck.

Fixed-Income Investment Index Fund (F Fund)   An F Fund is an investment fund that is for active and retired U.S. civil service employees looking for diversification in their fund that is low risk and provides capital preservation.

Front-end load fee   The sales charge or commission that an investor pays "upfront," or upon purchase of the asset.

Government Securities Investment Fund (G Funds)   This fund is for federal employees who have TSP accounts. It is considered low risk, has the lowest rate of return to date compared to the other funds, but it will never be a negative return.

Growth stocks   Stocks that are expensive relative to earnings as based on their price to earnings ratio, but the stock price is often justified by its high potential in the future.

Hard pulls   Credit checks that show up on your credit report and occur when you have given someone permission to view your credit report in order to get approved for a new line of credit.

Health Maintenance Organization (HMO)   An HMO is a health plan that limits a person's medical coverage to care provided by medical professionals who are in a contract with the insurance company and in facilities in the network of that HMO, focusing on maintenance and providing services that help promote wellness and prevent illnesses and diseases.

Health savings account (HSA)   An HSA is a medical savings account that has a tax advantage for those who are enrolled in a high deductible health plan.

High deductible health plan (HDHP)   HDHP health insurance plans have a higher deductible than traditional plans and the insured usually pays more for services provided before the insurance begins to cover the cost of the health care services.

Identity theft protection   Insurance to protect yourself from identity and financial theft.

Index fund   A mutual fund or exchange-traded fund designed to follow certain guidelines, so the fund can track a specified basket of underlying investments.

Individual retirement account (IRA)   This is an investment account that is not sponsored by an employer, so it is an investor's decision whether or not to open an IRA.

Individual service fees   These are additional administrative fees that cover features that you opt into, such as seeking financial advisory services.

Initial public offering (IPO)   An IPO is the process of offering shares or stock of a private corporation to the general public.

International Stock Index Investment Fund (I Fund)   An I Fund provides an opportunity to invest in non-U.S. companies rather than those in the Dow Jones Index and S&P 500 and, as such, is a good opportunity to diversify.

Large-cap stocks   Large-cap or large-market capitalization deals with companies that have a value that exceeds $10 billion.

Liabilities   Anything you owe is your liabilities, including loans.

Lifecycle Funds (L Funds)   L Funds are plans that are a mix of all the plans (G Fund, F Fund, C Fund, S Fund, and I Fund) and are similar to target-date funds, meaning that they are invested in growth assets.

Long-term care insurance   Insurance for those who are 55 years of age or older to help defray some of the cost of the care for the aging and/or disabled, including in-home care or care in a facility.

Long-term disability insurance   This is insurance that replaces your income in the event that you are unable to work due to an illness or an injury; it is a supplement to your lost income.

Management or advisory fee   This typically is a percentage of assets under management that the investor pays to a financial advisor or robo-advisor.

Market capitalization   This simply is the total value of the company stock within the actual stock market.

Micro-cap   Also called micro market capitalization, these are companies that have a value less than $300 million.

Mid-cap stocks   Companies that are in the middle range from about $2 billion up to $10 billion are all in the mid-cap or mid-market capitalization category.

Money market account   This is an account that is offered and insured by banks and credit unions, typically paying higher interest rates than other types of savings accounts.

Mutual fund   An investment that pools an individual investor's money with other investors' money to purchase shares of a collection of stocks, bonds, or other assets.

Net worth   This is the amount that you owe once you have subtracted (liabilities) from what you own (assets).

Point of service plan (POS)   A health insurance plan in which the insured typically pays less as provider care is provided by those affiliated with the plan's network and typically requires a referral from a primary care provider for any kind of specialist.

Preferred provider organization (PPO)   A PPO is a health insurance plan that allows the insured typically to pay less for all of the care providers within the plan's network but an additional cost for those outside the network of the health care providers and facilities. Generally the insured does not need to have a referral for those outside of the network.

Purchase fee   This fee that some funds charge is incurred by the shareholder when investors buy mutual fund shares.

Redemption fee   A fee paid to a broker that some funds will charge a shareholder when investors sell or redeem their mutual fund shares.

Risk tolerance   This is the acceptable level of risk an individual is prepared and able to accept.

Roth IRA   An individual retirement account (IRA) that allows the participant to save a designated amount of after-tax income money each year which then means the earnings and the withdrawals are tax-free after the person is 59½.

SEP IRA   This is similar to a SOLO 401(k) with a few exceptions. This plan is allowable for businesses with only one person employed or with a spouse.

Shares   Units of stock.

Simple interest This is the way of calculating the amount of interest for the principal amount of money, as based on a specified rate of interest.

Sinking fund A sinking fund is a fund or savings pot in which you periodically set money aside for purchases that you know are upcoming. This could be a vacation or wedding, for example.

Small-cap Companies with a market value that is less than $2 billion but generally greater than $300 million are classified as small-market capitalization companies.

Small-Capitalization Stock Index Fund (S Fund) This fund attempts to match the performance of the Dow Jones Index which is invested in small and medium-sized U.S. companies. The companies in the Dow Jones Index are those excluded from the S&P 500 Index. This fund has a higher change of volatility than the C Fund but there is more potential for higher investment returns.

Snowball debt method This is a debt paydown method that organizes your debts by listing debts beginning with those that have the least amount of debt to those with the largest amount of debt and paying them in that order.

Soft pulls These deal with credit and mean you have given someone permission to check your credit report, but they do not see your credit score.

SOLO 401(k) This is an investment plan for those who are self-employed, allowing the investor to maximize retirement savings, and contribute as an employer and as an employee.

Stock Owning stock in a company is ownership in it which includes its earnings and its assets. Owning stock entitles the stock owner to a portion, whatever amount of stock he or she purchases, of the business's assets and profits.

Target date fund These are investment products that automatically do the asset allocation and rebalancing for the investor, such as with a 401(k).

Taxable Brokerage Account This is an arrangement in which an investor deposits money with a licensed brokerage firm that places trades on behalf of the investor.

Testator   A person who makes a will is often denoted as the testator.

Thrift Savings Plan (TSP)   A contribution plan that resembles a 401(k) that is for U.S. civil service employees and retirees as well as members of the uniformed services such as the Army, Navy, or Marines.

Transaction fee   A fee for each time an order to buy or sell a mutual fund or stock is placed.

Trust   A legal arrangement for the transfer of legal assets from the owner, also called a grantor or a trustor, to the trustee.

Trust fund   A fund that is set up to hold assets such as stocks, bonds, mutual funds, real estate, hedge funds, and other valuables, such as art, that will be given to a person at a designated time.

Umbrella insurance   Insurance that is an extra layer of protection for assets not covered by regular insurance, protecting the insured in lawsuits, against injury to other people, and damages to other people's property. It is not a standalone policy but is in addition to an existing homeowner's policy.

Uniform Gifts to Minors Act (UGMA)   This is an Act that allows assets, such as securities, to be provided to a minor, so all possessions and control of the property are to be held in a custodian's name. An attorney is not needed to set up this type of trust fund.

Uniform Transfers to Minors Act (UTMA)   This is an Act that permits minors to own different types of property.

Value stock   Stock that is a low-priced stock to purchase relative to its earnings.

Vantage score   A person's credit score which is based on five categories: payment history, amounts owed, length of credit history, credit mix, and new credit,

Variable expenses   Expenses such as food and utilities that vary monthly are considered variable expenses.

Variable income   Income that is not *fixed* but changes for each pay period, such as side hustles and part-time work, where hours vary.

Will   A legal document that distributes a person's assets to his or her heirs and beneficiaries after the person's death as stipulated by the wishes of the deceased.

Zero-based budgeting   This is a method of budgeting in which all take-home pay earned is allocated to an expense, savings goal, investment goals, or debt payoff.

Resources

Chapter 2

Three-month lookback analysis tool: `https://docs.google.com/spreadsheets/d/1vNyQJfP9_IXWc709cN1Ldp1k0gtHtf5B/edit?usp=sharing&ouid=116139709658139381680&rtpof=true&sd=true`

Chapter 3

YouTube video about paying off debt first or investing first: `https://youtu.be/_vrkAIoKpCA`.

Compound interest calculator: `https://www.investor.gov/financial-tools-calculators/calculators/compound-interest-calculator`

Balance sheet: `https://docs.google.com/spreadsheets/d/1FOa-HecVY5zEuEtUrZPcRmcMzaLwcueF/edit#gid=768022440`

Chapter 5

Amortization schedule: https://docs.google.com/spreadsheets/d/
1sWNo95Uv--LAV5WNbxx3q1ARuxrRbssR/edit?usp=sharing&ouid=
116139709658139381680&rtpof=true&sd=true
Vertex 42 amortization resource: https://www.vertex42.com/Excel
Templates/excel-amortization-spreadsheet.html

Chapter 6

Portfolio allocation: https://www.youtube.com/watch?v=7ig1AEju0mM

Chapter 7

401(k) Rollover to IRA Free Service: https://capitalize.sjv.io/c/
3012883/1222600/13208
529 Plan information for each state: https://investor.vanguard.com/
tools-calculators/529-plan-tax-benefits-by-state
Charles Schwab Risk Profile Investment Questionnaire: https://www
.schwab.com/resource/investment-questionnaire
Vanguard Risk Profile Investments Questionnaire: https://investor
.vanguard.com/tools-calculators/investor-questionnaire#
modal-start-quiz
JP Morgan Risk Profile Investment Questionnaire: https://am.jpmorgan
.com/us/en/asset-management/adv/investment-strategies/
model-portfolios/explore-model-portfolios.
Investment calculator: https://www.calculator.net/investment-
calculator.html

References

Bessembinder, H., Labriola F., and Labriola, M.B. (2022) Do Stocks Outperform Treasury Bills | W. P. Carey School of Business. Retrieved July 6, 2023, from https://wpcarey.asu.edu/department-finance/faculty-research/do-stocks-outperform-treasury-bills

Betterton, R. (2023, March 3). States with the Highest Car Loan Balances. Bankrate. Retrieved May 30, 2023, from https://www.bankrate.com/loans/auto-loans/states-with-highest-car-loan-balance/

Black, M., and Frankel, R.S. (2023, May 22). What Is the Average Credit Card Interest Rate This Week? May 22, 2023. *Forbes*. Retrieved May 30, 2023, from https://www.forbes.com/advisor/credit-cards/average-credit-card-interest-rate/

Einstein, A. (n.d.). Quote by Albert Einstein: Goodreads. Retrieved June 8, 2023, from https://www.goodreads.com/quotes/76863-compound-interest-is-the-eighth-wonder-of-the-world-he

Federal Bureau of Investigation. (2022). 2022 Internet Crime Report. Retrieved from https://www.ic3.gov/Media/PDF/AnnualReport/2022_IC3Report.pdf

Franklin, B. (2006). *Autobiography of Benjamin Franklin* (F.W. Pine, Ed.). Project Gutenberg. www.gutenberg.org.

Franklin, B. (2023). Quote by Benjamin Franklin. Goodreads. Retrieved July 4, 2023, from https://www.goodreads.com/quotes/276870-little-strokes-fell-great-oaks

Gillespie, L. (2023, January 13). Average American Debt Statistics. Bankrate. Retrieved June 20, 2023, from https://www.bankrate.com/personal-finance/debt/average-american-debt/

Gusner, P. (2023, May 30). Average Cost of Car Insurance 2023. *Forbes Advisor*. Forbes. Retrieved July 7, 2023, from https://www.forbes.com/advisor/car-insurance/average-cost-of-car-insurance/

Hayes, M. (2023, January 18). What Is Emotional Spending? Experian. Retrieved May 30, 2023, from https://www.experian.com/blogs/ask-experian/what-is-emotional-spending/

Hudspeth, C. (2022). The Cost of Missing the 10 Best Days in the Stock Market. FMP Wealth Advisers. Retrieved July 6, 2023, from https://fmpwa.com/the-cost-of-missing-the-10-best-days-in-the-stock-market/

Lazy Portfolio EFT. (2023, June 17). Ray Dalio, All Weather Portfolio: ETF Allocation and Returns. Retrieved 28 June 2023, from https://www.lazyportfolioetf.com/allocation/ray-dalio-all-weather/ch7?

Longley, R. (2019, August 14). *Biography of Jacob J. Lew, Former Secretary of the Treasury*. ThoughtCo. Retrieved June 30, 2023, from https://www.thoughtco.com/jacob-lew-secretary-of-the-treasury-3322109

Phillips, B. (2023). Quotes by Bill Phillips. Goodreads. Retrieved July 4, 2023, from https://www.goodreads.com/author/quotes/731.Bill_Phillips

PNC Insights. (2021, January 4). Emotional Spending: Learn What It Is and How to Control It. PNC Bank. Retrieved May 30, 2023, from https://www.pnc.com/insights/personal-finance/spend/emotional-spending.html

Ramsey Solutions. (2023, April 12). The National Study of Millionaires – Ramsey. Retrieved May 30, 2023, from https://www.ramseysolutions.com/retirement/the-national-study-of-millionaires-research

Redemption Fee. (n.d.). Investor.gov. Retrieved July 7, 2023, from https://www.investor.gov/introduction-investing/investing-basics/glossary/redemption-fee

Schwantes, M., Locke, E., and Latham, G. (2018, June 13). Science Says Only 8 Percent of People Actually Achieve Their Goals. Here Are 7 Things They Do Differently. *Inc. Magazine*. Retrieved May 30, 2023, from https://www.inc.com/marcel-chapte2?schwantes/science-says-only-8-percent-of-people-actually-achieve-their-goals-here-are-7-things-they-do-differently.html

Van Knapp, D. (2017, February 13). What Is the Value of an Advisor? Vanguard Totes Up 'Advisor's Alpha'. Seeking Alpha. Retrieved July 7, 2023, from https://seekingalpha.com/article/4045415-what-is-value-of-advisor-vanguard-totes-up-advisors-alpha

Disclaimer

Please note that Budgetdog, LLC, is not a financial advisory group, nor do we claim to be. Budgetdog, LLC, does not provide investment or financial advice in any form and is not a broker. You understand and acknowledge that there is a degree of risk involved in any financial decision that you make. You acknowledge and agree that you, and not Budgetdog, LLC, are solely responsible for your own investments and research. The viewers who access the group should verify all claims and do his or her own research and due diligence before investing in any securities mentioned and are urged to confirm that data with the specific issuing company. Budgetdog, LLC will not be liable to any person or entity for the quality, accuracy, completeness, or reliability of any investment or informational source. Budgetdog, LLC, encourages its visitors to invest carefully and read the investor information available on the websites of the Securities and Exchange Commission (SEC) at www.sec.gov and/or the National Association of Securities Dealers (NASD) at www.nasd.com. You are responsible for your own investment and decisions, and you should obtain advice from a professional, prior to making any trade or investment of the type discussed or posted in the group. By using or accessing the group, you agree that you have read and understood this policy, and acknowledge and consent to the learning, collection, use and sharing of your information as described in this policy.

Index